Latinos at Work

Career Role Models for Young Adults

Careers in Sports

Valerie Menard

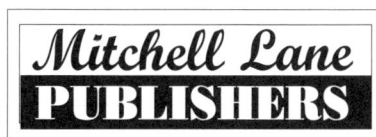

Mitchell Lane
PUBLISHERS

PO Box 619
Bear, Delaware 19701

PARKER HILL

Latinos at Work

Career Role Models for Young Adults

Careers in Community Service

Careers in Education

Careers in Entertainment

Careers in Law and Politics

Careers in the Music Industry

Careers in Publishing and Communications

Careers in Science and Medicine

Careers in Sports

Careers in Technology

Latino Entrepreneurs

Library of Congress Cataloging-In-Publication Data

Menard, Valerie.
    Careers in sports / Valerie Menard.
      p. cm.—(Latinos at work)
    Includes bibliographical references and index.
    Summary: Briefly presents the qualifications for and rewards of careers in sports, from athlete to publicist, and highlights the unique experiences of Hispanic Americans through profiles of successful Latinos in sports.
    ISBN 1-58415-086-6
    1. Sports—Vocational guidance—Juvenile literature. 2.Hispanic American athletes—Juvenile literature. [1. Sports—Vocational guidance. 2. Hispanic Americans. 3. Vocational guidance.] I. Title. II. Series.
GV734.3 .M46 2001
796'.023'73—dc21
                                                  2001042775

Careers in Sports

About the Author

Valerie Menard is a freelance writer. She was hired as an editor for Hispanic Magazine when the magazine moved from Washington, D.C. to Austin, Texas, in July 1994 and remained with the magazine through 1999, when it relocated to Miami, Florida. Before joining the magazine she was the managing editor for five years of an Austin bilingual weekly, *La Prensa.* At *La Prensa,* Valerie became an expert on the Hispanic market and an advocate for Latino causes. At *Hispanic,* she promoted stories that addressed the important political and social issues facing Latinos. As a freelance writer she has written for several publications including: *The Austin American Statesman, Estylo, Latina Style, Red Herring, Hispanic,* and *Vista.* She has also written biographical books for children as part of the *Real Life Reader Biography* series and in 2000, her first solo book project, *The Latino Holiday Book,* was published by Marlowe and Company. The book is in its fifth printing and the Spanish version will be published in 2002 by Random House Español.

Photo Credits

All photographs are courtesy of the person being profiled.

Acknowledgments

The profiles of success depicted in Part Two were all written from the author's personal interviews.

Publisher's Note

The careers depicted in this series are by no means all-inclusive. We have tried to show a representation of what is available by industry. Your career center at school or your local library can be of additional help identifying careers we might not have covered. The Web sites mentioned in this book were all active as of the publication date. Because of the fleeting nature of Web enterprises, we cannot guarantee that all sites will be operational when you are reading this book.

Contents

Part 1
Choosing a Career in Sports   **7**

Part 2
Profiles of Success   **29**

Part 3
Resources   **83**

Indexes   **90**

PART

1

Choosing a Career in Sports

· TABLE OF CONTENTS ·

Careers on the Playing Field

Athletic Trainer	9
Baseball Player	11
Baseball Umpire	12
Basketball Player	12
Boxer	13
Coach/Manager (Professional)	15
Coach/Manager (College, High School)	15
Equipment Manager	16
Football Player	16
Football Referee	17
Hockey Player	18
Jockey	18
Soccer Player	19
Softball Player	19

Careers off the Playing Field

Athletic Director	21
Manufacturer's Representative	21
Marketing Director	21
Personal Trainer	23
Professional Scout	23
Public Relations Director	23
Publicist	24
Sports Agent	24
Sports Attorney	24
Sportswriter	26
Sportscaster	26

Sports in the United States have focused for many years on three main areas: football, baseball, and basketball. Secondary sports such as hockey and soccer have received greater attention in recent years, but the world of sports is much more diverse than these five areas. These very popular team sports have been promoted because they have regular seasons (which usually don't conflict with each other), and they're well suited for television.

For Latinos, several sports have seemed more appealing than others, judging by the number of Latino athletes in those sports. Boxing, soccer, and baseball are where many Latinos have found careers. The reason may be that these sports are open to all children, whether they live in small towns or big cities. Across the country, most children can participate in some kind of city or volunteer league in these sports. Lately, more Latinos have emerged in sports such as football and even hockey. As the Latino population in the United States grows, more and more Latino athletes will be found in different sports. Census 2000 is projected to show that the Latino population has grown from 11 percent to 13 percent of the total population, and by 2005 Latinos are expected to be the largest minority group in the country.

Team sports may seem the most popular, but there are also several individual sports for children to pursue; many of these also provide more opportunities for girls. Sports such as track and field, swimming, diving, tennis, and bicycling require an athlete to dig deep to find his or her inner strength. Some schools offer programs with coaches and trainers and the potential for students to compete. For sports such as gymnastics or tennis, many children have to find programs offered by their city parks and recreation departments or even consider private lessons.

After high school, these individual athletes may want to continue to compete in order to be considered for the U.S. Olympic team. The U.S. Olympic Committee (USOC) is based in Colorado Springs, Colorado, but each sport has its own office based elsewhere. There are 296 events listed for the Summer Olympics; these involve 26 sports. In the Winter Olympics there are nine sports and 78 events.

Athletes who choose to become Olympians are some of the most respected in the world. Although some of the most successful athletes, like

Michael Thompson or Marian Jones, may get endorsement contracts (payment to appear in advertisements for companies such as Nike or Burger King), Olympic athletes, in general, earn a lot less money than professional athletes.

The cost and commitment of being an Olympic athlete is fairly great, but many athletes may move from an amateur status to a professional career. Oscar de la Hoya became a very successful professional boxer after winning the gold medal at the 1992 Summer Olympics in Barcelona. The International Olympic Committee has also relaxed its rules, which had previously blocked professional athletes from the games; this is no longer the case. Professional tennis, basketball, soccer, and hockey players are allowed to compete. Still, most Olympians are nonprofessional athletes, which makes the challenge of paying for coaches and travel to international competitions even greater.

Successful people follow their dreams. For the child who dreams of becoming an athlete, talent and determination can make that dream come true.

As a career, however, the jobs in sports are not just for athletes. For those who want a career in sports, there are other kinds of jobs available. Jobs such as coach, sportswriter or announcer, or umpire or referee may appeal to some. Other jobs such as agent, trainer, or scout will appeal to others. Even further removed from the playing field, sports careers can be found at the executive level, such as owners, or in other support staff positions, such as lawyers, managers, and administrators.

Selected Job Descriptions in Sports

Careers on the Playing Field

Athletic Trainer

One of the most valued members of a team is the athletic trainer. Trainers work with the athletes not only to make sure that they stay healthy, but also to assist them during a game if they are injured. Athletic trainers work with the other medical staff to diagnose a player's injuries and determine when that player will be ready to play again.

Most athletic trainers are required to have an undergraduate degree in physical education. Important courses to take include anatomy, nutrition, and

How Do You Know if a Career in Sports is Right for You?

Some parents encourage children to be athletic almost from the moment they start to walk. Exercise makes children strong and also teaches things like teamwork, cooperation, and organization, which is why children seem to be surrounded by sports. Mastering jump ropes, tricycles, and skates improve a child's coordination and balance. Games like hopscotch, tag, and Simon Says develop a child's competitive instincts, and at day care centers or in kindergarten, kids begin interacting with other children and playing team sports.

Most kids have some kind of athletic ability, but eventually the ones who show a special talent for a certain game start to emerge. Some kids will have great speed while others will have good agility. These children may join a team sport like baseball, football, or soccer, while others will pursue individual sports like tennis, gymnastics, or golf. They may begin to compete as an amateur or on the school team. For most professional athletes, this early training has been one of the keys to their success.

It takes a lot to be an athlete. Just enjoying the outdoors or being active isn't all that's required. The next thing most coaches look for is natural talent. Students with natural speed, agility, or strength will be encouraged to pursue athletics. It's up to the child, however, to decide what sport he or she wants to pursue. That decision is critical, because it reveals what the student enjoys, and love of the sport is almost as important as talent. It will give an athlete the added incentive he or she needs to push that much harder to succeed.

Another trait teachers and coaches look for is the love of competition. Something almost all athletes will say when asked why they are so successful is that they love to compete. Whether it's a track star who loves to race or a football player who hopes to win the Super Bowl, athletes love to compete. The desire to win can be as strong a motivator as the love of the game, and certain personalities will have that characteristic.

Once children discover that they have natural talent in a sport that they really enjoy, they need to set goals and focus on achieving them. Early training in any sport is essential, but the next step toward a career in sports is commitment. As athletes mature they begin to see sports as a career path, which will mean devoting more time and energy to athletics and planning to take the career to the next level from junior high school to high school, to college, and eventually to the professional level.

For children who love sports but just don't excel in any one activity, there are many more careers available behind the scenes. If they have writing skills, they may decide to be a sports reporter or commentator. Even kids who eventually become lawyers can still work in the sports industry representing athletes. There are many more opportunities for a career in sports off the playing field than on it.

first aid. Some college programs for athletic trainers have been accredited by the National Athletic Trainer's Association. Salaries for athletic trainers start at $23,000 and rise to $60,000 per year. Salaries are greater for trainers working with a professional sports team: $25,000 to $115,000 per year.

Baseball Player

Baseball players usually specialize in one of nine different positions—pitcher; catcher; first, second, or third base; shortstop; or right, center, or left field. Major League Baseball (MLB) is divided into to two leagues, American and National. All players are also bat-

ters except in the American League, which uses a designated hitter to bat for the pitcher. Most baseball players are not drafted out of college onto a major league team, but rather must get years of experience in a farm system. Players are drafted from college or recruited from other countries, particularly Latin America, and then trained for a time in the team's minor league, or farm, system. The majority of Latino players are recruited from the Dominican Republic. Minor league teams are divided into triple A, double A, or single A levels. The amount of time spent in the minors depends on the player's talent and health. If he's not injured and he excels, he will move out of this system and into the pros within a year.

There is no minimum age requirement for baseball players. Experience and talent are valued much more highly. Salaries range from $14,000 per year in the minor leagues to $25.2 million per year (that salary record was set in 2001 by shortstop Alex Rodriguez when he was signed by the Texas Rangers).

Baseball Umpire

Baseball cannot be played without umpires. There are four umpires on the field, the most noticeable one being the home plate umpire. There is also a first base umpire and third base umpire to determine foul balls and to call players safe or out at each base. The second base umpire calls the player safe or out at second base. The umpires also determine if a missed play was due to an error.

Umpires usually begin by judging amateur level baseball like Little League. Many consider umpiring a hobby and not a full-time job. There is no educational requirement, but umpires do learn about the job by attending a recognized umpire training camp or school. Once training is completed,

they begin their careers at the minor league level. Starting salaries for umpires begin at $25,000 per year.

Basketball Player

Basketball players are divided into five positions: one center, two guards, and two forwards. The guards provide the defense and the forwards the offense. There is no farm system for basketball players, so many are recruited into the pros right from college. Many earn college scholarships out of high school, which may require them to complete their academic requirements and earn a bachelor's degree before leaving school. Many times, however, the lure of professional sports takes players out of college before they complete their degree.

Basketball is not exclusive to men. The Women's National Basketball Association (WNBA) began in 1997, and international leagues for women have existed since basketball was accepted as an Olympic sport in 1976. There have been exceptions, but on the whole basketball players need to be tall, at least six feet. There is no minimum education requirement, although these athletes are more educated than most because of their college experience. Minimum salaries can start at $242,000 and

The "Golden Boy," Oscar de la Hoya

Oscar de la Hoya did not become a millionaire overnight, but it was almost that fast. Shortly after winning the gold medal for boxing at the 1992 Summer Olympics in Barcelona, Spain, de la Hoya signed the professional boxing contract that began his career.

Boxing had been a blessing and a curse for a young de la Hoya growing up in a tough East Los Angeles neighborhood. Those early days in the gym were difficult, but he learned how to protect and feel good about himself. Love of the sport and his family, especially his mother, inspired him to victory in Barcelona and in his professional success.

He still remembers what it was like to be afraid and to not have hope, which is why de la Hoya always valued his position as a role model. "I go back to schools to speak to kids about their futures," he said in *Oscar De Le Hoya,* a Real-Life Reader Biography from Mitchell Lane Publishers. "Just because they are Hispanic, they shouldn't feel left out or below someone else—we should all feel equal. I grew up without having anything in life: I had to struggle, so I can relate to them."

As a boxer, he initiated a scholarship program and helped pay for the renovation of a gym in East Los Angeles, which is now called the Oscar de la Hoya Boxing Youth Center. He has also offered to be a spokesman for several other causes, including the National Council of La Raza and the Hispanic Scholarship Fund.

can rise to $20 million or more per year. For women, annual salaries start at $30,000 and can reach $60,000 or more.

Boxer

Professional boxers emerge from city recreational programs or small, specialized gyms. In urban communities, boxing programs are developed as a means of keeping kids in school, as well as to help them develop a skill. Not surprisingly, most boxers have urban back-

Meet Tommy Nuñez, NBA Referee

Growing up in Phoenix, Arizona, Tommy Nuñez could not have cared less about his school work. All he wanted to do was play sports. He played baseball, basketball, and football. Although he would never compete professionally as an athlete, his love of sports would pay off when he became a professional referee in the NBA.

His road to this job was not an easy one. He was not just a poor student in school, he got into trouble early and was forced to choose between going to jail or joining the Marines. His life did settle down after that, but when he was first approached by the Phoenix Suns in 1970 to try out to be a referee, he wasn't sure he could do it. "At the time, I was too afraid I'd fail," he said in *Tommy Nuñez: NBA Referee/ Taking My Best Shot* from Mitchell Lane Publishers. "I didn't really give it any serious thought. Here I was at thirty years old . . . and these guys were talking about going to New York to try out for the big leagues. I said, 'No way!'"

Like most professional referees, Nuñez started his career at the amateur level. He was a referee for high school football, basketball, and baseball. He needed to earn extra money for the family, and it kept him close to sports, which he loved. He also worked as a referee for city leagues in Phoenix, for the parks and recreation leagues, and for the YMCA. Referees can earn $25 per game to start, but as a full-time job, they can get $100,000 or more per year.

It took Nuñez a year to think about it before he did decide to try out for the NBA. Of the more than 100 men who competed for the job, Nuñez was one of five to be chosen.

In basketball, the referee must be in very good shape. He or she must run up and down the court with the players. Referees must also be able to make quick decisions and stand by them. In basketball, it can be especially scary when a man more than six feet tall towers over you to argue a play. Tough to the core, that was no problem for Nuñez. "To be a successful referee you can't worry about being popular. You do need to have a reputation for being fair. We're like highway patrolmen. We don't catch all the speeders, but we get enough to keep the game under control."

grounds. There are numerous amateur leagues that feature boxers in all divisions, from light flyweight to super heavyweight. Fighters are classified by their weight at the amateur and professional level. A light flyweight must weigh at least 106 pounds but no more than 111 pounds. Many fighters train to make an Olympic team before turning professional, and many Olympic gold medalists turn out to be very successful professional boxers.

There is no education requirement, but boxers are expected to train rigorously and to accumulate a series of successful bouts before becoming professionals. A boxer will sign a contract with a professional boxing promoter, who will be responsible for arranging each fight. Payment for each fight is called a purse. First-time fighters may receive a $200 purse for a four-round fight. Successful fighters can earn multi-million dollar purses.

Coach/Manager (Professional)

Depending on the sport, the team leader, the person who inspires the players to victory and points out mistakes after defeat, is the coach or manager. Much like the word infers, coaches take a player's natural talents and put them together with the other talents from other players to form a successful team. Because it pays to win, professional coaching positions may not last long, forcing coaches to relocate several times before finding the right program or school.

Coaches aren't expected to be former professional athletes, but the majority have been athletes at one time. They hone their skills at the junior high and high school levels and on into the college level. On professional teams, some work their way up from the assistant coach level. Most have a bachelor's degree in physical education. Annual salaries for coaches at the pro level can start at $35,000 and climb to over $1 million.

Coach/Manager (College/High School)

Like coaches at the professional level, college and high school coaches must perform the duties of inspiring their players to victory and improving the talents of all the players to ensure success. Because these coaches will deal with athletes before they perhaps become professional, the burden is great to properly train and educate their charges. Also, at this level coaches may instruct more than one sport; at smaller schools, they may be in charge of all sports. Some coaches are also required to teach other subjects in the school.

College and high school coaches are required to have a bachelor's degree and in some cases a master's, usually in physical education. Since high school coaches are considered part of the faculty, an education degree is usually required. Salaries may range from $20,000 to $400,000 for college and $20,000 to $70,000 at the high school level.

Equipment Manager

People with mechanical skills who want to be close to a team may opt to become equipment managers. The main responsibility of the equipment manager is to make sure all the equipment required by the team, from helmets to hockey pucks, is in good working order for each game. If a piece of equipment breaks during a game, the equipment manager will be called in to fix or replace it.

Equipment managers are considered part of the team. They travel with the team and work on the playing field during games. There is no minimum education requirement, but many do belong to the Equipment Managers Association, which provides career guidance and support. Salaries depend on the sport and the size of the team. Equipment managers can earn $18,000 to $45,000 per year.

Football Player

A football team carries the most players of any sport. There are eleven offensive players, eleven defensive players, and eleven special teams players. Most football players are drafted out of college. Players who are not picked out of college can pursue careers in alternative leagues, particularly the Canadian Football League (CFL), then move over to the National Football League (NFL) in the United States. Players for some positions, such as place kicker, can come from entirely different sports, such as soccer.

There is no minimum education requirement, but since players are drafted at the college level, many do have an opportunity to complete a bachelor's degree. The minimum annual salary for a rookie player in the NFL is $131,000. Latino players have traditionally been hired as place kickers, but more and more they are surfacing as defensive and offensive lineman.

Meet Norberto Davidds-Garrido, Professional Football Player

Growing up in Southern California, Norberto Davidds-Garrido never dreamed he would be a professional football player, but he did know that he loved athletics. "I was always involved in some kind of sport. Actually, I started off in baseball and soccer," he remembers. It wasn't until he entered high school that he opted to play football. "I hadn't decided what I wanted; I liked all sports and I didn't know how to get there."

Turning his attention to football was obviously the right decision. As he matured, Davidds-Garrido grew taller—he now stands at six feet, three inches. He played defensive and offensive tackle positions. He did so well that he won a scholarship to the University of Southern California (USC) to play football for the USC Trojans. From there he was drafted by the Carolina Panthers in 1995. He has yet to make it to the Super Bowl, but the Panthers did make it to the playoffs one season. In 1999 he was traded to the Phoenix Cardinals.

Professional football is a tough sport. "There's a lot of pressure to win," admits Davidds-Garrido. But on those days when the team is successful, that is when Davidds-Garrido really appreciates the profession he chose. "When you do your job, pushing back the defense so that the offense can be successful, and the coaches recognize it, that's the best moment," he asserts. "Day to day, football is hard work, but Sunday is show time. That's the day for us to shine."

Football Referee

Professional football referees enforce the rules of the NFL during each game. There are seven on the field at a time: line judges who call a play in or out of bounds, field judges who call illegal plays and offensive or defensive infractions, and one referee who oversees them all. There are only sixteen games per team per season, which severely limits opportunities for referees. Many consider the job extra income.

Like other officials, football referees must train through amateur experience and then complete a licensing procedure administered by the Professional Football Referees Association. They must have 10 years' experience refereeing at the college football varsity level before applying to the program. Paid per game, referees can earn between $600 and $2,500. There is no other minimum education requirement, but referees must have good vision, good concentration, and quick decision-making ability.

Hockey Player

With over 26 teams in Canada and the United States, the National Hockey League (NHL) has brought this winter sport to areas that had never experienced it before, including California, Texas, and Florida. Each team has twelve players who perform offensive and defensive duties, depending on which team has control of the hockey puck. Like some other sports, hockey players are groomed through a farm system. Some may be drafted out of college, while others try out for the team. Players from both sources are placed on minor league teams to perfect their skills.

The first skill hockey players perfect is their ice-skating ability. Strong skating is a must in hockey. Athletes from parts of the country where the weather encourages hockey may hold an advantage over those who did not grow up with the game. Hockey players on a minor league team start at a salary of between $25,000 and $50,000. Professional players average between $200,000 and $350,000 per year. There is no education requirement.

Jockey

Jockeying is the perfect job for horse lovers. The jockey and horse must work together to win a race, and people who know and understand horses very well tend to have an advantage. Because there is a size limitation—jockeys shouldn't weigh more than 100 pounds—jockeys tend to be small in stature or very young, before they've grown to their full height. Some women have also entered the sport.

Many Latino jockeys, such as Angel Cordero, have made names for themselves in this sport. Most begin by working in the stables and caring for the horses. They may eventually get a chance to race. No minimum education is required, but when a jockey turns eighteen, he or she may apply for an apprentice license from a state or local racing organization to begin racing. Jockeys can earn from as little as $40 a race to $250,000 plus a percentage of the winnings.

Soccer Player

Major League Soccer (MLS) has seen its fan base grow incredibly since the World Cup (the Olympics of soccer, which takes place every four years) was held in the United States in 1994. Also, the success of the U.S. men's Olympic team and the triumph of the women's soccer team in the 1998 World Cup for Women have propelled the sport in this country. Soccer players begin as amateurs but go on to play at the college level and for semiprofessional teams.

Because the sport has yet to be accepted nationwide, salaries for professional players in the United States remain relatively low. They can start at $30,000 per year; the average annual salary for a player in the United States is $250,000. Female players with the Women's United Soccer Association (WUSA) earn between $25,000 and $80,000 per year. Some players will opt

out of playing for a professional team in the U.S. and pursue a team in Europe or Latin America, where the sport is considered a national pastime, on the same level as baseball in this country. There are no education requirements. Agility is especially valuable in this sport.

Softball Player

No female baseball leagues exist today, but softball allows for women to compete in a sport that is very similar. The positions are the same as those in baseball, but there is an extra outfielder. Other differences include a larger ball, underhand pitching, and aluminum bats rather than wooden ones. Softball has remained an amateur sport for a long time, but when the sport was accepted into the Olympics, international leagues developed and players began to make professional salaries.

Female softball players emerge from amateur leagues and college teams. Some join the newly formed Women's Professional Softball League (WPSL), while others pursue work in international leagues, which pay much better. Salaries for the WPSL range between $15,000 and $20,000 per year. Olympic gold-medalist Lisa Fernandez opted

What Are Some Benefits of a Career in Sports?

Athletes make great heroes. Whatever the sport, there are fans who consider it the most exciting game on the planet and its players the most admirable and glamorous people they know. It's not surprising then, that many children dream of becoming athletes. For some, the attraction may be the money, but for those who plan to play successfully, it's for the love of the game.

Athletes love to compete, and for them, sports provide an ideal work experience—they get paid to do something they love. The chance to compete, whether as a team member or as one athlete against another, is what athletes enjoy. Nothing is more thrilling than victory or more devastating than defeat, and for athletes, the process of achieving either result is thrilling.

It takes hard work to be an athlete, which may explain why athletes earn such large salaries. Talented athletes can become millionaires overnight. For many people, that kind of lifestyle is hard to imagine. Athletes live in style. Many own mansions and drive expensive sports cars. Their families also enjoy the comfort of an athlete's salary. They take the best family vacations, traveling to all parts of the world and staying in the best hotels.

Besides a good salary, being a sports celebrity has other benefits. Sports celebrities are considered role models, which is an honor and a great responsibility. Children look up to athletes, especially those who actively participate in different charities. For years the NFL has been known as a major supporter of the United Way, a nonprofit organization that gives money to social and education programs in different communities. For many, the opportunity to give back to their community is one of the biggest perks of being an athlete.

For nonathletes who work at different careers within sports, the opportunity to be close to something they love is a great fulfillment, whether it's as a food vendor or a sportscaster. They may not earn as much as athletes, but their careers may last longer and be just as exciting.

Success pays in sports, but achieving that triumph takes time and commitment.

to play in the Japan league for a while, where she earned $500,000 a year.

Careers off the Playing Field

Athletic Director

The athletic director for a city or university education system oversees the entire athletics program, from budget issues to personnel. He or she usually works at the district or university administrative offices and works with other education administrators to develop a broad physical education curriculum. The athletic director will hire coaches and physical education teachers for the district or university.

A physical education and teaching degree is required for this job, and a master's may be preferred. Athletic directors usually begin their careers as physical education teachers and then move over to the administrative side. Annual salaries can start at $20,000, depending on experience and the size of the school, and go up to $75,000.

Manufacturer's Representative

People who love sports and salesmanship will excel as manufacturers' representatives. These representatives must take certain products to sporting goods stores and sell them wholesale. The stores then sell the product to the consumer. Companies such as Nike, Wilson, and Reebok all employ manufacturer's representatives in order to get their merchandise to a store and eventually to the consumer.

Strong people skills and sales techniques are valued in this profession. Most companies require a high school diploma, but there are exceptions. Sales techniques can be improved through experience. Salaries are sometimes based on a commission (a percentage of the total sale), a straight salary, or both, and can range from $22,000 to $125,000 and up.

Marketing Director

On the business side of professional sports, the marketing director is in charge of a team's popularity, which many times is determined by ticket sales. To improve popularity, the marketing director must make sure that the team and its players are visible, accessible, and appealing to the fans. Gimmicks such as ball, bat, or hat day were probably designed by a marketing director and his or her staff. Placing advertisements on radio and television and in the print media is also the marketing director's responsibility.

Drawbacks of a Career in Sports

For the athlete, the main drawback of a career in sports is that it doesn't last long. Depending on the sport, an athlete's career can be as short as one week and as long as about fifteen years. Athletes may receive larger pay than most people, but their careers are also the shortest.

Athletic competition takes a huge toll on an athlete's body. A healthy body is essential for any athlete. An injury can end a sports career in seconds. Even if athletes manage to avoid injuries, as people age, they naturally start to slow down. Very few athletes continue to work past the age of 40.

Opportunities as an athlete are very limited. The number of jobs available is extremely small compared to the number of athletes who are looking for a chance to play professionally. In her book *Career Opportunities in the Sports Industry,* author Shelly Field lists several different jobs in sports, but for the team sports, she notes that the chances of getting a job are "poor."

For Latinos, the limitations are sometimes greater. Preconceptions about a Latino athlete's abilities may keep recruiters away when it comes to sports like hockey or basketball, but they will come to predominantly Latino high schools in droves looking for baseball players. NBA players like Eduardo Nájera and NHL player Scott Gomez are breaking these stereotypes.

For nonathletes, the number of jobs is still limited. Not every city has professional teams, which tend to offer the best salaries. There are still careers in sports, but they will be found in less glamorous settings.

This position requires a bachelor's degree usually in an area such as marketing, business administration, public relations, communications, or journalism. Marketing directors should have good people and communication skills. Annual salaries start at around $25,000 and can go to $150,000 or higher.

Personal Trainer

Exercise does not always come easily for some individuals. To help with their motivation and to find the right exercise regimen, many people hire personal trainers. The personal trainer gives the client instructions on how to use different exercise equipment and programs to maximize their effects. Trainers also provide some nutritional advice.

Because personal trainers charge a fee, the more clients they have, the better. The most successful trainers will utilize their knowledge of health and exercise to produce positive results for their clients. There is no minimum education requirement, but a degree in physical education will provide an important credential to clients. Trainers charge per session; fees can range from $25 to $500 or more.

Professional Scout

College recruiters look at high school athletes across the country to decide which ones merit a university scholarship. At the professional level, scouts do the same for a team, but their search for the best athlete can take them to other countries. The professional scout performs all the research on an athlete, as well as evaluates the athlete's skills, before bringing him or her to the attention of management.

Professional scouts travel constantly. There is no minimum education requirement, but many do have a bachelor's degree. Many are former athletes, coaches, or trainers. Scouting requires a complete understanding of the sport combined with a natural ability to spot talent. Annual salaries range from $20,000 to $100,000 or more.

Public Relations Director

The position of public relations director involves some of the elements of a marketing director, like promoting a team's image, but the public relations director will do this by dealing more directly with the public and the media. When journalists call to set up interviews with athletes, they will deal with the public relations people. At the same time, if any internal situations arise with a team, such as hirings or firings, the public relations director will take this information to the media. Complaints from fans will also be dealt with in this office.

A bachelor's degree in communications, public relations, marketing, or sports administration is require. Good communication skills are also essential. The annual salary for this position starts at $40,000 and can rise above $125,000.

Publicist

On the way to becoming a public relations director or marketing manager, many people start out as publicists. Working with the public relations manager, the publicist will write press releases dealing with issues or events regarding the team. The publicist will comply with information requests from reporters and will help schedule interviews with athletes. He or she makes it a point to be familiar with local and national media figures in order to get publicity for a team.

Most publicists have a bachelor's degree, but some former athletes have been hired as publicists as well. It's more likely, however, that publicists will start out as journalists or sportswriters and then make the move to working for the team. Salaries range from $20,000 to $100,000 per year.

Sports Agent

The professional scout many times represents the team. When he or she spots an athlete they wish to approach, they must deal with the sports agent, who represents the athlete. Sports agents will negotiate with the team on behalf of the athlete in order to get the best deal. Many times they will take a percentage of their client's salary as their fee, so agents tend to seek the highest possible salary for their client. Since the more money their client makes, the more they make, agents will also acquire endorsement deals (where the athlete appears in an ad or commercial) for their client.

Since salaries are based on a percentage of an athlete's salary, agents tend to earn a lot from the start, especially if they have more than one client. Earnings range from $200,000 to over $750,000 a year. A college degree is not required (although many agents do have law degrees), but experience in sales does help. Above all, agents must have great people skills and be excellent negotiators.

Jose Massó: Never on the Sidelines

Jose Massó of the Center for the Study of Sport in Society warns students not to focus exclusively on careers as athletes. "For many, it's unrealistic. The number of positions available on any team for an athlete is so limited. There are many more opportunities to work in the field of sports, but off the playing field," he advises.

Sports lawyers have become especially important in the field of sports. Contracts have gotten so complicated that unless an agent has a law background, many athletes refer contract negotiations to their lawyers rather than to agents, explains Massó. "Jobs off the playing field offer us an opportunity to be near athletes but in a different capacity," he says. "There is a great need for Latino entrepreneurs to work in the field from parking managers to ticket sales; there are many more money-making opportunities behind the scenes in sports."

The Center for the Study of Sport in Society began 19 years ago at Northeastern University in Boston, Massachusetts. With a staff of researchers, the center looks at what role sports plays in society— what benefits they bring and where can they be improved. It has produced several reports from this research.

One of the most famous reports, *Racial and Gender Report Card*, dealt with the amount of money Latinos earn compared to non-Latinos. When the report was first published, Latinos made up a very small percentage of the number of athletes in certain sports, like basketball, but a very large percentage in other sports, like baseball. The number of Latino managers and coaches, however, was very small.

The Center will publish an updated report in 2001. The results will also be posted on its Web site, www.sportinsociety.org. "We're starting to close the gap, but we still have a lot more work ahead of us," says Massó.

Sports Attorney

Because player contracts have gotten so complicated, many athletes have dropped their agents and increased their legal support. Since the nature of the work is seasonal, few law firms specialize in sports law, but they may devote certain members of their staff to deal with these issues. Besides negotiating contracts for athletes, sports attorneys can also represent a sports facility during licensing disputes and a sports team when it has trademark problems.

This position requires a law degree and passing the bar exam. It also requires research to find the law firms that deal with sports teams and players. For the aspiring sports attorney, the effort will be worth it. Starting annual salaries for any lawyer begin at $40,000 and can reach well over $400,000 for law firm partners.

Sportswriter

The best writers write about what they know. Consequently, most sportswriters are sports fans who may not have had the talent to be an athlete but have a love of sports and a talent for writing. Sportswriters work at print publications such as local newspapers, and many cover local sporting events such as high school games. In larger cities, sportswriters are assigned to a beat to cover professional sports. They not only attend and take notes at games, but they also must secure interviews with players, coaches, and general managers.

Sportswriters should study journalism and acquire a bachelor's degree. Depending on the size of the publication and the city in which it's located, sportswriters can earn from $15,000 to $85,000 per year.

Sportscaster

Like sportswriters, sportscasters should love sports. Many on network television are former athletes, but on the local level, sportscasters are people with degrees in television journalism who decided to specialize in sports. Sportscasters begin by reporting from sports events and after a few years can earn a position as sports anchor, reporting the scores and sports events of the day during the local news broadcast.

On a national level, sportscasters may specialize in a certain type of sport or level of competition. Many report exclusively on college football, soccer, or golf, for example. A bachelor's de-

Olympic athletes many times convert gold medals into a professional career.

gree in journalism is not required but is strongly encouraged. Sportscasters must have excellent writing skills. Salaries can start at $18,000 and rise as high as $1 million for network positions.

PART 2

Profiles of Success

TABLE OF CONTENTS

Linda Alvarado, Baseball Team Owner (New Mexico) 31

Lisa Fernandez, Softball Player (California) 37

Tom Flores, Football Coach (California) 43

Carlos Girón, Sports Publicist (New York) 51

Alex Gonzalez, Baseball Player (Florida) 57

Carlos Llamosa, Soccer Player (Florida) 63

John Ruiz, Boxer (Massachusetts) 69

Brenda Villa, Water Polo Player (California) 75

Linda Alvarado

Baseball Team Owner

Being the first Latino in any field is a little scary. It's called "breaking new ground," which means that a Latino is going into an area where no Latino has gone before. Linda Alvarado had already broken new ground when she decided to start a Hispanic, women-owned business in the construction industry. At the time, a woman on a construction site was not very welcome. Years later when she, along with a group of other investors, decided to purchase a major league baseball team, she knew that she would become the first Latina as well as the first Hispanic to ever own a professional team in any league, and she was ready for it.

"I grew up with five brothers and no sisters," explains Alvarado, "so I was always involved in sports. I grew up participating in team sports. My father played recreational softball and I played softball; I wanted to be like my dad. During an inning he would let me run out and sweep home plate clean. It's very emotional to me to think how things have come full circle. Now he can sit in the front row behind home plate and watch a game."

While she was growing up she had limited financial resources, but as a business owner, she earned the money required to purchase a team. Alvarado also says that the fact that baseball is one of the few professional team sports to have a large number of Latino athletes on the roster encouraged her as well. "Latinos make up 38 percent of all the players in major and minor league baseball, so it was with great pride that I got involved in a sport where Latinos excel," Alvarado asserts.

She was also in the right place at the right time to buy a baseball team. The Colorado Rockies and Florida Marlins were the first two expansion (new) teams allowed in Major League Baseball (MLB) since 1976. The Rockies and Marlins were added in 1991. Purchasing an established team is difficult, explains Alvarado, but with an expansion team, interested buyers submit bids to MLB that include incentives for MLB to bring a team to their city. Incentives can include building a brand-new stadium at no cost to MLB, giving MLB a percentage of ticket sales, and an initial investment of nonrefundable cash up front. At the time that Denver, Colorado, (home of the Rockies) submitted a bid, there were five other cities interested. The group of seven owners in Denver included local business leaders. Alvarado was the only woman, as well as the only Hispanic.

"This was a high-risk venture," reveals Alvarado. "If you look at the population of Denver, there were many cities bidding with more people than we had in the entire state. Our bid was predicated [based] on a plan that we would become a strong regional team and attract fans to our stadium from Mexico to Canada." Denver is also home to three other professional teams: the Nuggets in basketball; the Broncos in football; and the Colorado Avalanche in hockey.

MLB looked at all the bids and narrowed the choice to two cities, Denver and Miami. All the other bidders lost their up-front cash deposits to the league. Only certain people can write a $1 million-plus check and be able to lose that money, so Alvarado was in a very rare position. "It was a high-risk venture, but also a once-in-a-lifetime opportunity, not available to the majority of men, much less women."

Still, becoming a baseball owner involves more than money, suggests Alvarado. Besides the financial investment, a successful team must have in place a strong organization that includes a strong general manager, an experienced manager, experienced talent scouts who can recruit the best players, and a good coaching staff that can bring a team together. Finally, a love of the game is also essential. According to Alvarado, "The best thing about owning a professional baseball team is the sport itself. As a contractor I build schools, airports, convention centers, and high rises. It's a lot more fun to go to a game on a summer's evening," she relates.

No baseball team can be successful without fans. Alvarado and her partners knew that they needed to reach beyond Denver to fill a stadium. They began by working on the team's image. To do this, players were encouraged to reach out to the community by volunteering and working with community groups. Alvarado says this approach not only worked, it was the right thing to do.

Today, the Rockies still make an effort to be present in the community. "We have a charitable foundation focused on literacy, and with the players' involvement have helped build baseball fields throughout the city to keep kids focused on events that will keep them aligned with succeeding in school," says Alvarado. She regularly invites local schoolchildren for tours of the team's facilities. They get a chance not only to meet the players, but also to see how many people it takes to put a team together and how many different jobs there are off the playing field. As an added perk, Alvarado gives front-row seats to a home game to local children who perform well in school. "This helps the children see themselves as important people. I want them to dream of becoming athletes, but also of possibly starting a business that's related to sports, like in the marketing, broadcasting, and hospitality fields, and coming back to work with the team," she says. "I feel it's important to motivate young children to become leaders, not just for one day, but also to see themselves as our future leaders."

There are challenges to owning a professional team, admits Alvarado, and the biggest and most obvious one is the expense. There is no salary cap (maximum amount a team can spend on salaries) in baseball, which is why players still make headlines when they sign huge, multimillion-dollar con-tracts. For teams in big cities with large television markets like Los Angeles and New York, it's easier to lure players away from smaller teams with the promise of a huge paycheck. In smaller markets, explains Alvarado, the challenge is to find those talented young players, in college or the minor leagues, and sign them before a larger team gets to them. That way the players can be groomed by the Rockies. If they become baseball stars, they may opt to stay in Denver after their contract expires. If not, these young stars will have kept the team competitive within its division.

Besides the players, there are other expenses associated with running a professional team. Says Alvarado, "It's a challenge to stay cash positive, but on the other hand all sports franchise teams have appreciated [grown] in value over time and most owners have made a significant amount of money."

She says she realizes that owning a team is a dream for many Hispanics and hopes that many more will have their dream come true. Her own dream is that MLB will begin to look at expansion teams in Mexico and other Latin American countries. The league already has two teams based outside the United States: the Montreal Expos and the Toronto Blue Jays in Canada. "This southern expansion would create the opportunity for more Latinos to own teams," she says.

Although she'll only admit that her investment as a part-owner of the team was a multimillion-dollar one, Alvarado agrees that the number of Latinos in that kind of financial position may be limited. Still, she's confident that as the number of Latinos increases, so will the number of opportunities. "Latinos have not lacked ability," she says, "but they have lacked opportunities." Besides being successful entrepreneurs, Alvarado advises that future team owners should also have a high profile within the community. "Becoming involved in your community will elevate your profile. You not only have to be able to take the risk and write the check, your involvement with team ownership has to bring credibility to it. MLB looks for those things."

Alvarado was born during the 1950s in Albuquerque, New Mexico. Growing up with brothers may have also encouraged her to seek a type of business that was unusual for women. According to her, however, it was a great unplanned career. As a college student she worked in a botanical garden. From this experience she realized that she liked working outside. Her next job was as a contract administrator at a construction site. She remembers that although she wasn't entirely welcomed by the men she worked with, she still thoroughly enjoyed that job.

She did complete her undergraduate work in economics, but she also decided to take courses that would help her in her job, such as estimating, surveying, critical path scheduling, and running computer and software programs related to the construction industry. "This additional education was critical," asserts Alvarado. "It enabled me to develop skills many men, who had been working in the construction industry for years, didn't possess, like computer expertise."

Over time, she says, she began to consider owning her own general contracting firm. Construction contracting is still very much a man's world. For the most part, contractors submit bids to a private, city, county, or federal agency for construction work. Architects design a building, but the general contractors actually build it. They don't all build buildings, however. Some contractors are called subcontractors because they specialize in a certain area of construction and perform work for general contractors. This is how

Alvarado started. "Some of my first jobs were curb and gutter projects," she says.

At first many of her bids got rejected. She began to use her initials and not her full name on bid proposals so that it wouldn't be obvious that she was a woman, or as she puts it, "so that I wouldn't be immediately eliminated." That seemed to work, and Alvarado began to get contracts (jobs). "At the time I dreamed of one day building high rises," she says. "Today, Alvarado Construction builds high rises. We even built Invesco Field at Mile High, the new Broncos stadium. It's important to be committed and take your hopes and dreams seriously. You should embrace them and find ways to turn them into reality."

The key to her success, she feels, is partly due to the influence of her parents, Lily and Luther Martinez. They enabled their six children to develop confidence. Her brothers are Luther, Lavern, Le Roy, Lawrence, and Lemuel. Lily and Luther supported Linda's career choice even though it was nontraditional. "They had to try to explain to their friends that their daughter was a contractor," says Alvarado. "They taught us to have pride in our heritage and advised us that we may experience bias but that was no reason not to try."

Luther is a second-generation Mexican American from California. Lily traces her family roots back to when the explorer Francisco Coronado first brought the Spaniards to the Southwest, at least five generations ago.

Confidence may seem hard to come by at times, but Alvarado asserts that it is the key to success. "It's important that one believe in oneself even when others may not," she says. From personal experience she knows that she persevered, even though she was told repeatedly that she didn't look like a contractor. Many things in her life would not have happened if she lacked confidence, including becoming the owner of a baseball team. "I had to convince myself that I could succeed before I could convince anyone else," she says. "If I had been narrow in focus and believed the myth that women could only be secretaries or that Hispanics could only be laborers rather than successful business owners, I would never have been able to achieve my dreams. In my career, I took the path least traveled and it made all the difference."

Linda Alvarado is making a difference for Latinos in Colorado and across the country. She was the first Latino professional team owner, and by setting the example, more will follow.

Lisa Fernandez

Softball Player

Becoming an athlete was inevitable for Lisa Fernandez. Since both her parents were athletic, it was in her genes as well as in her environment. She was born and raised in Southern California, where for many, spending time in the park or at the pool was a daily ritual. For Fernandez, "It wasn't a question of whether I was going to become an athlete, but more, which sport would I choose." In the end, she chose softball.

When she was a child, her parents, Antonio Fernandez and Emilia Padilla, regularly took Lisa and older sister, Elsie, to the park. As former athletes, they encouraged their daughters to play and have fun. "Basically they said, 'Here it is. Find something you enjoy.'" Fernandez feels that it was important that her parents encouraged her very early on to be athletic. "They kept exposing me to different sports; any sport I wanted to play, they encouraged me. I had good hand-eye coordination and I liked playing catch. I also played basketball and tennis and participated in sports clinics. After a while, softball was the sport I gravitated to."

At times the whole family got involved, which was usually a good thing but sometimes spelled disaster. Fernandez remembers one time when, at the age of 11, she was pitching in a girls' fast-pitch softball game and her grandmother caused a commotion. She had decided to cut across the field to reach the snack bar rather than walk through the stands. She made quite an impression with her lavender-colored hair. The umpire stopped the game until her grandmother was safely across the field.

In his native Cuba, Antonio Fernandez played on a semiprofessional baseball team. Emilia Padilla, of Puerto Rican descent, grew up in New York, and there she played stickball. In 1961, just after the Bay of Pigs (a failed attempt by the United States to invade Cuba and oust dictator Fidel Castro), Antonio emigrated to the United States from Cuba. He and his friend drove across the country from Miami to California. Emilia Padilla and her family also eventually moved to Los Angeles. Fate would have it that Antonio and Emilia would end up in the same neighborhood. "You could say my dad was the boy next door," says Lisa Fernandez.

Her parents worked hard to raise Lisa and Elsie. Antonio worked as a foreman in a factory. Emilia stayed at home with the girls, but as they grew older she ventured back into the workforce as a teacher's aid. When the company Antonio worked for went bankrupt, Emilia took a job as a secretary at St. Anthony's Church to support the family. Lisa saw this as a little girl and believes that it was her parents' hardworking example that has helped her today. "My parents gave me a great work ethic. If you really want something, you'll do whatever it takes to get it, including working very hard," she says.

Fernandez was born February 22, 1971, with, she admits, an athletic ability and natural skills. "God gives us all talents, we just have to discover what those talents are and go for it. If someone's an artist, he or she might not want to sit in a park and play catch, they would prefer to be in a room and draw a beautiful picture. An accountant loves numbers and a performer loves standing in front of people and being the center of attention. Everybody has something in life that they enjoy doing and are good at. That's the endeavor we should take. It should be the pursuit that we enjoy so that we will work harder at it to be the best we can be."

For women, the world of professional sports is much more limited than it is for men. Only recently have professional team sports leagues like the Women's National Basketball Association (WNBA) and the Women's United Soccer Association (WUSA) evolved. There is no professional baseball league for women, but the Women's Professional Softball League (WPSL) is about to start. For Fernandez, this league is way overdue. "We've been waiting for a professional league for so long. All I really want to do is play. I'm hoping this league will give me and other members of [Olympic] Team USA that opportunity," she says.

The lack of opportunities to play is the biggest challenge for Fernandez. Few softball players can make a good salary from playing professionally unless they play overseas. When she played in Japan, she earned nearly half a million dollars. A starting annual salary for a WPSL player is $25,000. But money isn't everything, and because she missed her family, Fernandez returned to the United States. Until she can find work on a professional softball team, Fernandez volunteers at the University of California at Los Angeles (UCLA) as an assistant coach.

One of the things she loves most about the sport is competing. Playing against another team constantly pushes Fernandez to test herself mentally and physically. In the 2000 Summer Olympics in Sydney, Australia, Fernandez, who starts at third base when she's not pitching, grabbed a lot of media attention after the team turned to her and she practically willed them to win. "I live for the opportunity to get the game-winning RBI or make the diving play with the bases loaded," she told one reporter. Shortstop and fellow Latina Crystal Bustos made her debut on this Olympic team.

Ranked the number one team in the world and being the gold-medal team from the 1996 Summer Olympics in Atlanta, Georgia, Team USA was highly favored to win the 2000 gold medal in softball. But as the Olympic tournament began, Team USA, the powerhouse, became vulnerable. They lost three games, one to Japan, one to China, and the other to Australia. Not only was this the first three-game losing streak for the team in the sport's 35-year history, it also put the team in the position of having to win all five of the remaining games to repeat as gold medal champions. At the time, Fernandez told *Sports Illustrated,* "This has been the biggest mental challenge I've faced in my career. But I'm confident we'll all break through it." Even coach Ralph Raymond commented to *Sports Illustrated,* "I never thought I'd see a whole team go into a swoon as far as hitting and scoring. We don't seem to be the same team we were a week ago."

The team almost felt cursed, so in a symbolic attempt to "cleanse" the team of any bad vibes, Fernandez suggested that they all get into the shower together, in their uniforms, for a "voodoo cleansing." Whether it was the shower that gave the team a psychological edge or there really was a curse is unclear, but the team changed after that and went on a winning streak all the way to the gold medal round. According to Fernandez: "We scrubbed off the evil spirit that was on us."

It was Fernandez who pitched successfully in the gold medal game against Japan. "When I'm on the mound I have tremendous focus," said Fernandez in *Latina Style* magazine. "I want to make the [ball]. If we're going to win or we're going to lose, I want it to be while I have the ball, because I'm going to prepare to the best of my ability to make sure that things come out on the right end."

Ironically, Fernandez never planned to be an Olympian. When she began playing softball, the sport was not part of the Olympics, so she never dreamed she would be able to participate in the Games. That changed in 1995 when softball became an Olympic sport for the first time and Team USA won its first gold medal when the sport premiered at the 1996 Summer Olympics. Softball was an immediate hit among the fans. Richard Hoffer of *Sports Illustrated* wrote at the time that scalpers (people who buy tickets to an event and then resell them at higher prices) were getting $300 per seat for the gold medal softball game between the U.S. and China, and that throughout the tournament the U.S. games sold out. "Women's softball—like women's volleyball and women's soccer and women's basketball—took these Olympics by storm," concluded Hoffer.

"As an athlete, that's what you strive for, to be the best in the world," explains Fernandez. "That's what you compete for. That's why I get up at seven A.M. and lift weights and get on a bike. While other people are sleeping, I'm working. I do this because I've got to be prepared for challenges. If they weren't there, the game wouldn't be any fun. It's one thing to get to the top, it's another to stay there. That's what makes Team USA strong. We continue to push ourselves even though we're considered the best in the world."

Although she never expected to play in the Olympics, she would never trade either experience in Atlanta or Sydney. She also hopes to make the 2004 Olympics in Athens, Greece, where the Olympic Games began. "By being an athlete I've done things I would never have been able to do. I've gotten to travel and see the world, I've met people and learned new skills, especially how to communicate. I've learned life skills that will help me become a better person," she asserts.

The key to her success, she says, has been the work ethic instilled in her by her parents. When she's not training for the Olympics, Fernandez begins her day at 7:00 A.M. with an exercise regimen. She lifts weights and then rides a stationary bicycle until 8:30 A.M. She then goes to the gym for another workout from 9:30 A.M. to 10:30 A.M. After that, she drives to UCLA, where she's an assistant coach. "When I get there, I'll usually take some swings in the batting cage and then work with a couple of the pitchers." She'll continue coaching until 3:30 P.M. She gets home by 5:30 P.M. and tries to spend time with her family or, if she gets the urge, plays a few rounds of her second sports passion, golf. She goes to bed between 10:00 and 11:00 P.M.

Her family support has also been a key to her success, she says. They dedicated themselves to helping her achieve her goals, which involved some personal sacrifices of their own. They also gave her choices. She wasn't expected to do just girlie things but to do what she enjoyed. "I was lucky not to be raised with the traditional expectations of many Latinas, to become a wife and mother," she explains. Besides her family and hard work, Fernandez admits, "I was also blessed with a lot of God-given talent."

Another early motivator for Fernandez was a pitching coach's advice to her that she could never become a successful pitcher because her arms were too short. Naturally competitive, Fernandez took his advice as a challenge to prove him wrong, which she did. "My parents taught me that the only person who can limit you is yourself, and if you want something bad enough you have to work hard," she offers. For young Latinas who may decide that softball is their sport, Fernandez ad-

vises, "Never be satisfied. Always continue to try to accomplish your goals and remember to surround yourself with people who care and can help you achieve your dreams."

This advice can come in handy in a sport that is still growing. Athletically, almost anyone who wants to play the game can. For young Latinas with the physical talent and commitment to the sport, softball can be a great career. "It all depends on the effort you're willing to put forth and the sacrifices you're willing to make," Fernandez says. "This sport has tremendous opportunities. You don't have to be a certain size or height and there's no education requirement, although it's a good way to get a college degree through a sports scholarship." Fernandez is five feet six inches tall and weighs 175 pounds.

Parents and their children must work together to make sure that any athletic talent is not wasted. For Fernandez, she had parents who appreciated her abilities and also knew what it meant to be an athlete. Their insight, combined with Lisa's talent, helped create this softball superstar.

Tom Flores

Football Coach

Football fans hope for the chance to go to a Super Bowl game in person. Players and coaches begin each season hoping to win a spot in the playoffs and eventually to be one of two teams to compete for the title of best in the world. Coach Tom Flores not only got a chance to experience that dream, he lived it twice as the head coach of the Oakland and Los Angeles Raiders in 1981 and 1984, respectively.

This accomplishment is even more impressive when Flores admits that he never intended to be a coach. As a football player and student at College of Pacific (COP) in northern California, he pursued his education as strongly as he did athletics. "As an undergraduate and graduate student, I was preparing to go into teaching after my playing career ended," asserts Flores. He was a quarterback, the first Latino to hold that position in the NFL, for the Oakland Raiders from 1960 to 1970.

Flores was born the younger son of migrant farmworkers. His parents, Tom Cervantes Flores and Nellie Padilla Flores, were employed to pick crops in the field. As the younger Tom Flores describes in his book *Fire in the Iceman:* "My family traveled from crop to crop in California's hot, lush, central valley. We picked whatever needed to be picked. We were like thousands of Mexican-American families then and now."

Times were rough for the Flores family, which also included his older brother, Bob. During these times, as the coach tells it, he had no idea how poor they were, since he had never experienced anything else. Some farms had better living quarters for the workers than others, but Flores particularly remembers the first time the family lived in a house with bathrooms on the inside. This house was on a ranch outside of Sanger, California. Flores calls Sanger home, because this was where the family quit working in the fields, bought a small grocery store, and built a permanent home.

Once the family stayed in one place, Flores began to notice how different the schools were. They were much bigger and had a lot more kids. He attended Wilson Grammar School in Sanger and recalls the moment that football came into his life. He and a friend, Manuel Martinez, were walking home from school one day when they found a weird-looking ball. It was pretty ragged, it even had holes in it, and it wasn't round. Flores explains that he knew what a football was but had never actually picked one up. Manuel urged Tom to throw it, and when he did, it was like magic. "It spiraled perfectly as it arched through the air, then nosed into the ground about twenty-five yards away. . . . When I threw a football for the first time, that's how I felt—fascinated and challenged," he writes in his book. "If it had fluttered end over end and flopped on the ground a couple of yards away, maybe my whole life would have been changed."

Football became very much a part of his life from that moment. He played several positions on the football team at Sanger Union High School. He also played baseball and basketball, was in the school band, and became involved in school politics. In his senior year he was assigned to play starting quarterback. He began to look at colleges and set his sights on Stanford University, which had produced legendary football players. But when he spoke to his coach, Flores realized that he didn't have the grades to get accepted. He opted instead to go to Fresno Community College and from there transferred to COP. It proved to be the right decision. "If success is the product of being in the right place at the right time, then for me, the College of Pacific was the right place and 1956 was the time," he asserts in his book.

COP offered Flores a positive college experience—it's also where he met his wife, Barbara. Although he had a good college career, Flores was not drafted by any National Football League (NFL) team. A change in equipment at COP, namely shoulder pads, left his body vulnerable, and consequently he injured his shoulder. For this reason he was passed over through 30 rounds of the draft. One scout, who worked for the Canadian Football League, did approach him. Flores's first football contract was with the Calgary Stampeders. That was short-lived, however, and Flores had to return home to Sanger.

He chose to return to school to work on a master's degree. He also played football for a semiprofessional team. He earned only $50 a game, which meant he had to find a regular job. He worked at a pizza joint and also started coaching at COP. It wasn't until the American Football League (AFL) was conceived in 1959 that Flores was given a chance to play. The AFL began as an alternative to the NFL—there used to be two separate leagues. Cities like Dallas and Oakland had been denied franchises (new teams) by the NFL, so several entrepreneurs who wanted to start football teams in other cities got together and formed the league.

Flores had had shoulder surgery to fix the injury he'd suffered at COP and was invited to try out for the Oakland Raiders of the AFL. On July 11, 1960, he was one of 11 quarterbacks to show up at training camp. Two weeks later he became the starting quarterback. He played in the AFL for 10 years. During that time he was an Oakland Raider, a Buffalo Bill, and a Kansas City Chief. In 1970 the NFL and AFL merged into one league.

After retiring from football in 1970, Flores was approached by a friend to consider a job as the offensive coach of the Buffalo Bills. His friend was stuck without a coach and the season was about to begin. Flores agreed to do it, "as a favor," he says. "I got on a plane at midnight headed for Buffalo, [New York]." As a first-time professional coach in the NFL, Flores describes this experience as a "trial by fire." He admits, "We didn't win many games that year, maybe one or two, but that was because we didn't have a good team.

All of a sudden I was the offensive coordinator [coach] in the NFL and I had never coached before."

After one season with the Buffalo Bills, Flores returned to his home in Lafayette, California. He and Barbara had three children during this time, twins Mark and Scott and daughter Kim. In 1972 he interviewed with John Madden, the head coach of the Oakland Raiders, and was hired as an assistant coach. When Madden retired in 1979, Flores was made head coach.

The first season, Flores had to adjust to being head coach. His first assignment was to fire a veteran player and good friend Fred Biletnikoff. Certain players were still loyal to the old coach, others wanted to be traded to other teams. Everything eventually worked out, and by the next season Flores hoped to improve the team's record. It started off a little bumpy, however.

The team lost several games at the start of the season, and at one point Flores thought he might get fired. Slowly the team turned around. Jim Plunkett became the starting quarterback after the other quarterback was injured. When the team finally made it to the Super Bowl and had to face the Philadelphia Eagles, whom they beat 27–10, they felt they had earned it. "In one season we had gone from being the maligned [criticized] to the magnificent, from the valley of despair to the peaks of celebration. We were Super Bowl champions," writes Flores.

After that win, owner Al Davis decided to move the team from Oakland to Los Angeles. However, legal battles over the move prevented it for two years. Finally, on August 29, 1982, the team played its first game as the Los Angeles Raiders. The year after winning the championship, the Raiders did not return to the Super Bowl. Several players were injured, including Plunkett. There was also the controversy over the move. A losing season can sometimes have a happy ending, however. In football, the teams with the worst record one year get to pick first during the NFL draft. Flores took advantage of that and chose running back Marcus Allen.

Although the 1982 season began with strong victories for the Raiders, it stopped when the players went on strike (quit playing) in order to negotiate better working conditions from the league and the owners. The strike lasted 57 days. When it was over, the Raiders won several games and made it to the playoffs. At the start of the 1983–84 season, Flores hoped to get the team to yet another Super Bowl. He got his wish. The season went smoothly, and on January 22, 1984, the Raiders met the Washington Redskins in Super Bowl XVIII.

Everything clicked for the Raiders that day. Plunkett completed several passes to his favorite receiver, Cliff Branch, including one for a touchdown. The defense, lead by defensive end Lyle Alzado, intercepted a pass for a touchdown, and Allen scored a touchdown with a 74-yard run. "In 1980 we had a good team that played great at the right moments. But the 1983 team had much better talent, a truly great team," sums up the coach.

Coaching is considered one of the toughest jobs in professional sports. The pressure to win is tremendous because the blame falls more heavily on the coach than on the players. A player will get blamed for poor performance or a mistake on the field, but the coach will get blamed for a losing season. Because professional sports is a business, unsuccessful coaches don't last long in this profession. Flores was a winning coach, but he still admits to having to deal with a lot of pressure. "You either win or fail," he says. "Unfortunately, you could be a great coach or even a good coach and still get fired because you didn't win enough games. The pressure sometimes is unbearable."

Flores retired from the Raiders in 1988, but a year later he was back in football when Seattle Seahawks owner Ken Behring hired him to be president and general manager. At that time Flores became the highest-ranking Latino in the NFL. Three years later he stepped into the coaching position. There were great expectations in Seattle. With a coach like Flores, who had taken the Raiders to two Super Bowl victories, the Seahawks could have the same success. Unfortunately, that would not be the case.

Although the team had a respectable record during Flores's time there, the Seahawks did not make it to the play-offs, much less the Super Bowl. Before one game of his last season as coach, Flores was quoted as saying to the players: "I hope we can turn this around a little bit before the end of the season. If not, there could be a lot of changes. I could be one of them."

Despite the pressures of having to win, Flores says he loved his job, mainly because he loves football. As a player, it was just exciting to get the chance to play. As a player and coach, the thrill and excitement of a Sunday game made all the hard work worth it. "For me it's the game. We prepare 365 days a year for a twenty-four-day season," he says.

Flores feels that he was effective as a coach because he approached the job as a teacher. Rather than yell at the players, he concentrated on improving each player's performance by focusing on technique and training. "There were moments when I got angry, but if you blow your stack every day, sooner or later it becomes meaningless [to the players]," he says.

Flores preferred to keep his approach consistent. This method also helped him keep his cool during games, which is essential for making the quick decisions the game requires. "During a game, you might have five seconds to react, which can determine whether you win or lose," he asserts. "It's not like in the regular business world where you can say, 'Let me sleep on that.' I've got to make a decision, right then and there."

Flores remains one of the few Latino coaches to work in a professional league. Still, he believes that coaching is an open profession for Latinos, if not at the pro league level, then at the college or amateur level. The most important requirement to become a professional coach, he says, is a college education. Coaches rarely advance from the college level to the professional level without a degree, unless they're former professional players. Flores is both a former player and college graduate.

For the most part, Flores explains, coaches have to start at the college or high school level, and that will require a bachelor's degree in physical education and a teaching certificate. This type of training is important, he says, because "a coach is a teacher; that's what you're taught in school. I chose to be more of a player's coach than a strict disciplinarian. There are other ways of coaching, but I won two Super Bowls my way."

For years Latino players were very rare in the NFL, but in the 2000–01 season there were 12 players and three assistant coaches. The players may someday become coaches, and the assistant coaches may move to head coach positions. In order for the NFL to become more diverse, Latino players must be recruited from college, but before that can happen, "Latinos must stay in school and go to college," says Flores. "College recruiting in Latino-dominant schools does help, but you're not going to get recruited as a twelve-year-old. Many Latinos drop out of high

school at age sixteen. That's our biggest problem."

Besides going to college, Flores believes that to be successful as an NFL coach a person needs a good knowledge of what it takes to be a player. That usually comes from being a player, but Flores adds that a love, desire, and tremendous passion for this game is also important. "Good coaches have to be willing to learn, practice, and work hard," he says. NFL coaches today can earn up to a million dollars per season.

There is no time clock in the NFL, says Flores. During a season, coaches will work extra hard, but even during the off-season there's a lot of work to do. As he remembers it, during the season his days would begin at 7:00 A.M. Each day of the week was devoted to either recovering from the previous or preparing for the next game on Sunday. For instance, on Monday, he would start the day at 6:00 A.M. to review the previous game on film and prepare for an 8:00 A.M. meeting with the other coaches. At 1:00 P.M. the players would arrive. The coaches would take them through a workout until 4:00 or 5:00 P.M. Flores would continue to work until 10:00 P.M.

Tuesday was a day off for the players, but for Flores, it was his longest day, lasting until midnight. It would be filled with meetings and strategy sessions for the next game. On Wednesday and Thursday the players would return for more meetings and practice. Friday was devoted to reviewing the previous game and correcting any problems and also assessing the upcoming game and the opponent's strengths and weaknesses. Saturday would be devoted to reviews or travel if the Sunday game was out of town.

With all the pressures and challenges of coaching in the NFL, winning seasons for any coach are a great accomplishment. To make it to two Super Bowls in nonconsecutive years is even more amazing. Flores attributes his success to several factors, the first being the strong organization behind the Oakland Raiders, from the executive level down to the equipment managers. The second is that he had great players to work with, including quarterback and fellow Latino Plunkett, and running back Allen. Plunkett was named Most Valuable Player (MVP) of the 1981 Super Bowl, while Allen claimed the MVP title of the 1984 Super Bowl. Finally Flores believes his ability to stay calm despite all the pressure was also important.

After all this time, Flores still treasures his Super Bowl memories. It feels great to accomplish a goal, but for most people it's rare to have the opportunity to do this in front of thousands of fans and live on television. Sporting events seem to increase the thrill of the moment, so it's not surprising that Flores looks back fondly on his two Super Bowl victories. "There's nothing like that moment when the game winds down and suddenly you're the world champions and you look on the sidelines and see grown men crying. I have flashbacks about that. Nothing takes the place of these warm moments," shares the coach.

For children who hope to become athletes or coaches, Flores warns, "This is a very committed profession. It's very honorable and not one you go into just for the monetary reward. The most important question to ask is, do you love the game?" There will be rewards along the way, he says, but considering the time and commitment required, it may not always seem worth it. That's why a love of the game is so important. It will carry people through the tough times, like team losing streaks or getting fired. "If you have a passion for the game, then go for it," he advises. "If not, look for something else."

Carlos Girón

Sports Publicist

Like baseball in the United States, soccer is considered the national pastime in most Latin American countries. From Mexico to Brazil, kids there grow up with a passion for the game. Born in Guatemala City, Guatemala, Carlos Girón was no exception. He played soccer at an early age. "I was passionate for the game," he remembers. But soccer wasn't his only passion. He also loved to write, and as fate would have it, he excelled in one more than the other. Today he's the director of Hispanic communications for Major League Soccer (MLS) and says, "I have a dream job."

In Guatemala, his favorite soccer team was the team from the capital city called Municipal, or Los Rojos ("the Reds"). Girón explains that he liked Los Rojos because it was considered the team of the working-class or regular people. When he came to the United States, it was clear that baseball was the most popular sport here, but he quickly found a team to root for, the Cincinnati Reds.

Born November 10, 1965, Carlos Girón emigrated to the United States from Guatemala in 1978, when he was 12 years old. His father, Antonio, first moved to New York, and then years later his mother, Ruth, followed. While his parents were in the United States, Girón was raised by his grandmother, Maria Elena. His grandmother gave him a lot of confidence, he remembers. "She was my inspiration. She used to call me *el presidente,* 'the president,' because she said that I was going to be the next president of Guatemala. She seemed so certain that I believed her, and it wasn't until I was in college that reality hit and I thought that it might not happen after all," he says.

His parents, he says, "brought us here hoping to find more opportunities for better employment and education." When Carlos and his younger brother, Sergio, finally joined his parents, however, they learned that they had separated. His father eventually moved to Rhode Island and rarely, if ever communicates with his sons. "It's kind of ironic," says Girón. "My father loved soccer, and here I am working for the largest soccer organization in the country and he probably doesn't even know it."

Ruth Girón started working as a housekeeper and supported Carlos and Sergio. Carlos eventually went to college, where he chose to study journalism. Although he loved playing soccer as a kid, he realized that his real talent was as a writer. He attended the State University of New York at Albany and eventually graduated in 1988 from the State University of New York College at New Paltz.

Although he had earned a degree, Girón remembers that he still lacked confidence. "I lost my focus. I didn't know what I wanted to do," he says. "I did a variety of things. I worked in a hotel for a while and as a paralegal. I was trying to decide what I wanted to do, and then I remembered that I had been the editor of the college newspaper, that I was a good writer, and that I needed to be in a communications field."

He also remembers getting some very important advice about this time. Carlos ran into a photographer friend from Chile, Guillermo Torres, and showed him his clips (articles). "He liked them and told me that I should have no fear and I would be successful," says Girón. At his first press conference after a boxing match, however, Girón says that he was very nervous and intimidated not only by the other reporters but also by the athletes. "My friend told me not to be in awe of the athletes but to do my job and ask the questions. With his advice, I gained confidence, and the rest was easy."

He landed a job as a sportswriter for *The Jersey Journal,* and for the next three years, "I covered community sports and eventually some professional games. In 1996 I started covering soccer, namely, the New Jersey Metro Stars of the MLS." When *The Jersey Journal* launched a Spanish-language version of the newspaper, Girón was named sports editor. He wrote stories in both English and Spanish for the next three and a half years.

While covering soccer, he made a lot of connections with important people within the sport. They advised him of an opportunity in communications for the soccer governing body for North America, Central America, and the Caribbean called CONCACAF. He was in charge of all media with this organization. After two years he was recruited by the MLS to work in the league's communications department.

In his current position as director of Hispanic communications, Girón feels pretty fortunate. For someone who has loved the sport for so long, the opportunity to promote the game in the United States among Latino fans amounts to getting paid for something he enjoys doing. His main responsibility is to keep Hispanic media and sports journalists informed about any developments in the league, including competitions and news about the players. "Since I love the sport, it makes it like not having a job," he adds. "It beats working for a living."

Because soccer is so popular among Latinos, Girón also has an advantage over his colleagues, who must promote the sport in mainstream, English-language media. Soccer in the United States has grown a lot in popularity, especially since the World Cup of Soccer was hosted by the United States in 1994. The World Cup of Soccer is like the Olympics. It takes place every four years and is hosted by a different country each time. During the 1994 games, the U.S. team produced one of its strongest performances, and later it went on to win a bronze medal in the Olympics in Atlanta. Soccer in the United States took off. Its popularity continues to grow, especially with events like the World Cup. In 1998 the first World Cup of Soccer for women was held, and the American team actually won.

Still, getting newspapers and magazines to cover soccer in the United States is a challenge for most publicists. For Girón, the opposite is true. "I have such a variety of Latino media outlets, from television networks like Univision and Telemundo to radio shows, to daily and weekly newspapers, to magazines. My challenge is not to promote the sport of soccer itself; rather it is to promote the MLS brand of soccer. U.S. Hispanics have not yet fully embraced MLS," he says.

Girón also has more freedom in his job than publicists who work with mainstream media. When a publicist produces a press release (a rough story that gives reporters most of the facts with which to begin their own story), it has to be approved and edited several times. When Girón produces a press release, he says, he doesn't have to simply translate the English-language one, he can write his own release from a completely different angle so that Latino media will find it interesting. For example, if he produces a press release with statistics from a game, he will highlight the performance of Latino players. "I customize all MLS information to meet the interests and requirements of Hispanic media," he explains.

One downside to his job is having to deal with so many different people. Publicists are constantly talking to reporters and editors, trying to get them to publish a story. If they do run a story, many times the publicist will have to set up the interview and supply the reporter with additional information. In the end, if the story has errors or criticizes the team or player, the publicist can get blamed for bad publicity. "Some media outlets are never satisfied," he explains. "They always ask for more service and are very hard to please. That can be frustrating." The other downside to his dream job, says Girón, is that he has to travel during the season with the team, which takes him away from his family. He and his wife, Natalie, have one son, Alfonso, who is eight years old.

Still, Girón admits he is well paid, so that helps make up for the tough times. He earns a salary that is competitive with his colleagues in soccer, as well as with those in other sports such as baseball and football. Publicists for a professional sports team can make a starting salary of about $35,000 and can earn as much as $200,000, he asserts.

Education is essential to this position, but Girón believes it's essential for anyone, no matter what he or she chooses to be. As a publicist, however, getting a journalism degree does help students develop writing skills, and internships help even more. Like other talents, writing can be learned and can be improved with practice. Some colleges have communications departments that offer a public relations degree, but if not, a bachelor's degree in a related field—English, liberal arts, journalism, communications—is a requirement in this job.

For Latinos who might want to pursue this field, Girón believes that it is very open, "especially if you have strong communication skills." Besides a bachelor's degree in journalism or some kind of communications field, a prospective publicist, particularly one involved in sports, should acquire some experience as a reporter. "Writing for a newspaper or some kind of media outlet improves not only your writing but also your interviewing skills," he says. Also, a good understanding of the sport and a command of soccer terms and lingo is important.

For Latinos who have maintained their bilingual skills, the potential to be hired as a professional sports publicist targeting Latino media is especially promising. Girón contends that he uses both English and Spanish in his job on a daily basis. "It helps to be bilingual, but it's a challenge, especially in this country. You tend to focus on English and little by little neglect Spanish. For those who make the effort to keep Spanish, and can speak, read, and write in it, they will excel in a position such as mine," he says.

Publicists have to have good social as well as communication skills. Writing the press release is important, Girón stresses, but because publicists deal so closely with the press, they not only have to make the release interesting, they also have to satisfy the client, which is the media. "It's a combination of giving good information and getting along with others, and giving a good impression of the team to the media and the public," he says. His education and upbringing have given him the tools to manage these duties.

Girón hopes to continue in this field and to advance. "I see myself taking on a bigger project in sports, but it will also have to do with the Latino community," which is very important to him, he says. His job may not be as glamorous as an athlete's, but Girón is a pioneer in his own way. He's fairly sure that he is the only communications executive among all the professional sports leagues, including base-ball, football, and basketball, that focuses on the Latino press in the United States. Other leagues may have communications staff who deal with Latin American press, but Girón's job is unique.

The key to his success, he believes, is linked to his experience in college and his education. He would never have gained those early clips to show to his friend the photographer if he hadn't worked on the school newspaper and gotten his degree. Second, he advises, it's important for children to be confident and to believe in their abilities. His own lack of confidence almost kept him away from his "dream job," so he knows how important confidence is. For reporters or writers, confidence should increase with experience. Girón adds that knowing what you want early on will also help. "Determine exactly what you want to be and then go after it with no fear," he says. "If you don't have confidence, you'll be paralyzed. You'll have no motivation to do anything. Prepare yourself and focus on what you want."

Girón is living proof that his advice is sound.

Alex Gonzalez

Baseball Player

● ●

Many young boys in the United States dream of playing professional baseball. It's called "the national pastime," which means that baseball, more than any other sport, is considered the most popular and historically important sport in the country. That may be why so many young boys eagerly begin the road to that dream by playing T-ball and later joining a Little League team. Growing up in sunny Miami, Florida, Alex Gonzalez was not unlike most American boys. The only difference is he became one of the very few whose dream actually came true.

Gonzalez has been the shortstop for the Toronto Blue Jays for the past six years. He was so skilled as a teenager that he joined the team out of high school at the young age of 18, rather than out of college like most players. He was not immediately placed on the major league team, but played on a minor league farm team for the Blue Jays to help develop his talent. Gonzalez admits that it wasn't the easiest move he's had to make. "You could compare it to sending your kid off to college. Luckily, training camp was in

Florida, so my parents took me. It was very emotional," Gonzalez shares.

He did encounter a familiar face at camp, which helped. Chris Stein had played against Gonzalez in high school. Having someone at camp who was the same age and from Miami made the transition a little easier. Stein has moved on to play for the Boston Red Sox.

Although baseball is the national pastime of the United States, it is also very popular in Latin America. For countries that are especially close to the United States, baseball competes with soccer for popularity. Less than 100 miles from the Florida Keys, Cuba has been strongly influenced by this country, and baseball's popularity there is evident. In the Olympics, the Cuban team rivals Team USA as the favorite to win the gold medal. Team USA and Cuba have won two championships each since the game was introduced at the Olympics in 1984 as a demonstration sport. Baseball became an official medal sport in 1992.

Gonzalez says that part of the reason baseball was encouraged in his household was his father's love of the game. Born in Cuba, Guillermo "Bill"

Gonzalez would accompany his grandfather, Ricardo, to watch the Cuban national team play. In 1961, after the Cuban revolution, Gonzalez and his family moved to the United States. Alex's mother, Patricia Smith, met Bill Gonzalez by accident. Raised in Orlando, Florida, she went to Miami to visit a friend. It just so happened that Bill was also visiting a friend who lived at the same apartment complex. The two met and the rest is history.

Bill Gonzales eventually became a professor of engineering at the University of Miami, but he never lost his love for baseball. He continued his grandfather's tradition by taking young Alex to watch the University of Miami baseball team compete. "I was brought up around baseball my entire life," says Alex.

Alex Gonzalez was born in Miami on April 8, 1973. At age five he began playing Little League. The games were played at a ballpark in Miami called Flagami, which was located in a part of the city with a large Latino population. Gonzalez believes that playing with those kids improved his game. "The level of competition was really high there. Latin kids seem to develop faster," he explains. "It helped me to establish my skills because the competition was at such a high level."

His only sibling is his older sister, Donna. Without brothers to hang out with, Gonzalez developed friendships with a group of about eight or nine boys in the neighborhood. They all shared a love of the outdoors and athletics, which Gonzalez also feels helped keep him focused on becoming an athlete. "Every day we had some kind of sports team going, from baseball to basketball to football. That helped me learn to enjoy playing for the love of the game. It wasn't pressure for me. It was just going out there and having a good time," he says.

Gonzalez attended Killian High School and, as a sophomore, tried out for the baseball team. Usually underclassmen, sophomores and freshmen, are placed on junior varsity teams to give them a chance to develop as athletes. Gonzalez was an exception. "I surpassed my peers to make the varsity team. No one had even heard of me, but coach Pete Hertler really gave me every opportunity to succeed."

Gonzalez performed so well in high school that by his senior year he was receiving offers for a sports scholarship from three colleges—North Carolina State, Florida State, and the University of Miami. "I had it narrowed down to the Florida schools," Gonzalez remembers. "I wanted to stay close to my father so he could see me play. In the end I chose the University of Miami because it was like a dream come true, since I had watched them play since I was young." But when the Toronto Blue Jays offered to sign him directly out of high school, Gonzalez's plans changed.

He never attended the University of Miami. The call of the major leagues was just too strong. If he had gone to college, he thinks he would have been a science or accounting major. Gonzalez explains that his decision to pass on college was based on several factors. Injuries are always a threat to an athlete, and he had an opportunity to move to the major leagues while he was young and healthy. Also, because his father was a faculty member at the University of Miami, Gonzalez knew that he could always return to that university to get his degree and that his tuition would be paid for—faculty members can have tuition waved for their children. "I still think that education is very important, and if baseball can get you a college degree, that's a great thing," he adds.

Alex stayed in the minor leagues for three years and was moved to the major leagues in 1994. But he suffered a back injury that year and had to return to the minor leagues to recuperate. He rejoined the Blue Jays in 1995 and has been in the starting lineup ever since.

As a shortstop in baseball, Gonzalez says there are many skills that need to be developed, the least of which is batting. "Even if I were to hit twenty home runs in a season but I missed a lot of defensive plays, I wouldn't be a shortstop for long. The team would move me to another position," he admits. Getting the right training early is extremely important, because a player who hasn't been properly trained can suffer an early career-ending injury.

Agility is extremely important for a shortstop, so Gonzalez says he has focused on improving his footwork. Shortstops have to react quickly in order to keep a hit from reaching the outfield, and then throw the batter or runner out. Gonzalez jumps rope to increase his foot speed. He also concentrates on leg strength. Using weights to increase his leg strength helps him as a batter as well as a fielder. The most important requirement for a shortstop or for any of the infield positions is to be consistent. Players who routinely make defensive plays will be successful.

With 162 games in a season, Gonzalez keeps his skills sharp by practicing every day. Baseball does have the longest season in professional sports, but that gives players a little more time each day to relax. During the season and for home games, Gonzalez says he arrives at the ballpark at around 3:00 P.M. The first thing he does is work with a trainer on his legs, which he calls a "treatment" to loosen up. At 4:40 he begins his warm-up exercises to loosen his arm. He prepares for batting practice by first taking swings off a T, then he heads for the batting cage. He stays there about fifteen minutes. After that, he'll spend another fifteen minutes catching ground balls.

Practice usually ends between 5:45 and 5:50, which gives the players an hour and fifteen minutes before the game starts. He takes that time to look at scouting reports about the opposing players. The report tells him what kind of batter each player is and even how he tends to bat against a certain pitcher. In this way, Gonzalez can anticipate where the batter will hit the ball during the game. "It's made a big difference," he says. "I've learned over the years what certain hitters will do with certain pitchers. That way, I'll be in the right position so that I can make that play. It helps me make a play look a lot easier."

His favorite part about the game is the competition. "I always love to compete. The thrill of winning, that's the thing I've always known about the game. I like to go out there and try to win," he states. Gonzalez has also enjoyed the chance to travel and see other parts of the country. He's learned a lot about his fellow Americans, which he appreciates—especially one particular person. "I met my wife, Samantha, while traveling," he admits.

Traveling, however, can also be a burden on an athlete. Now that he's married with one son, Tyler, and another child on the way, Gonzalez would be happier to be at home than on the road. While his son grows older, Gonzalez knows that he's missing out on important moments. "Traveling makes it tough. It keeps me away from my family," he relates. "It's tough to know that I'm missing out on certain aspects of that part of my life."

Becoming a professional athlete in any sport is difficult, but of the three major sports in this country, baseball is also the most inclusive. Many of the greatest players in the sport, past and present, have been Latino. People still remember players like Roberto Clemente and, more recently, slugger Sammy Sosa. Over 30 percent of the league's players are Latino, and this is even more evident when watching a game. Latinos are still rare at the executive level of the game, but on the playing field, baseball has become a multiethnic sport.

There are more Latin American players in the game than U.S. Latino players, but Gonzalez believes that Latinos are heavily recruited by colleges and given an opportunity to move up to the major leagues. There is a large number of Latino players at the college level, asserts Gonzalez. In Miami especially, "Latin players are making a big impact in college. I don't know what the percentage of Latin players is from the U.S., but I do know that they are recognized as talented and are given opportunities, especially in college."

Baseball players earn some of the biggest salaries in professional sports, but Gonzalez cautions that it's important to remember that only a very small number will make it to the professional level. Most players start out in the minor leagues, where they will earn a monthly salary of between $800 and $1,500. If a player does move up to a major league team, the starting salary is $200,000.

For children who hope to play professional baseball, Gonzalez says it helps to focus on more immediate goals, like developing as a player in high school in order to get to college rather than focusing on playing professionally. The goal shouldn't be to play professionally only, but rather just to play. "Kids should really enjoy the journey of getting there," he says. There are so many variables, from injuries to playing behind a veteran that never allows a player to be asked to the major leagues. Getting a college scholarship from the sport is a great goal, he asserts. "I still believe that getting your education is very important. It gives you something to fall back on if baseball doesn't work out. I passed on mine, but my circumstance was very unusual."

With a long career ahead of him, Gonzalez will continue to inspire youngsters to play baseball. Latino players have made important contributions on the playing field. Eventually Gonzalez, or any of his colleagues, may move into management or coaching positions and make the game a national pastime that truly reflects its multiethnic fans and roots.

Carlos Llamosa

Soccer Player

When Carlos Llamosa was a little boy growing up in a small town in Colombia, he always dreamed of playing soccer professionally. At the time, however, it seemed hard to imagine. Many other things enter a boy's world when he lives in a country with the economic and political troubles that Colombia had and still has. Llamosa, however, also had the love and support of his family, which included 10 siblings and his parents, Alberto Llamosa and Lola Perafan. At the age of 21, Carlos followed his mother, four sisters, and five brothers and moved from Palmira, Colombia, to New York City. Llamosa never imagined that he would have a near-death experience there and that it would inspire him to make his dream come true.

"It was a dream for me to play professionally. I could never say that I would be a soccer player, because you never know, so many things can happen in your career," says Llamosa. For example, he had been playing soccer on semiprofessional teams in Colombia, but when he came to the United States in 1991, he says he stopped and never thought he would play again.

Concerned more with helping his family than pursuing his dream, Llamosa began working as a janitor in the World Trade Center, the two tallest buildings in the city at that time.

At noon on Friday, February 26, 1993, he and a few friends left the building to cash their paychecks and grab some lunch. On any other day they would have stayed and eaten lunch in the building. About twenty minutes after they left, they heard a huge bang. "I thought that the [subway] trains had crashed," he said to a reporter for the *Washington Post.* It turned out to be a bomb that had been left in a van and parked at the World Trade Center. The bomb killed six people, including a friend of Llamosa's, and injured more than 1,000. "We could have been in there," Llamosa told the reporter. "I think it was the luckiest day of my life."

This event may have helped Llamosa rethink his goals. "Every day I thought the bomb would explode again," he remembers. Although he continued to work as a janitor for a while longer, he also began playing soccer in city leagues, including the most powerful one, the Pan American League. In 1995 he tried out and was hired to play on a minor league soccer team, the New York Centaurs. "We had a great season that year. That's when I knew I could play professionally in the U.S.," he says.

He began his career in Major League Soccer (MLS) in 1997, playing for D.C. United, based in Washington, D.C. Llamosa tried out for the MLS in 1996 when the league began, but when the Los Angeles Galaxy offered him a contract for only $24,000 a year, he decided to wait. One year later, D.C. United picked him up. He performed well with the team but suffered injuries in 1998. In 2000, he was traded to the Miami Fusion. He also plays on the U.S. senior national team, which he considers an honor. Some players are chosen from the senior national team to compete in the World Cup and the Olympics.

His love of the game is clear. When asked to find a negative aspect, Llamosa responded that he really couldn't find anything bad about it. He doesn't mind traveling, and the pay scale is competitive, he says, between $30,000 and $500,000 a year. "I'm doing what I love, that's the most important thing, to do what you love and love what you do. Some people may be teachers but want to be something else but have to do that job. Sometimes people go into business but don't want to be businessmen. I always wanted to be a soccer player and I get paid for that. I'm making a living, raising a family, because I'm a professional soccer player. I have so much fun playing soccer," he continues. "Playing every day, practicing, I'm doing what I wanted to do since I was a kid."

Llamosa is also excited to be playing soccer in the United States at a time when the sport is growing tremendously. Salaries for professional players have improved because of this, and the prospects of playing the game as a career are now possible in this country. Much of that progress began when the biggest soccer event in the world, the World Cup, was played in the United States in 1994. Like the Olympics, the World Cup takes place only once every four years and in a host country. Between each cup, national teams compete in tournaments, and at the end of four years, 32 teams from around the world with the best records are chosen to compete.

In the past the United States rarely qualified for the cup, but because it was the host country for the 1994 games, it was automatically admitted. The games were also shown on television throughout the tournament, and the U.S. national team rose to the occasion. Normally defeated in the first round, the national team managed to make it to the second round and competed aggressively in the loss to a soccer powerhouse, the national team from Brazil. U.S. fans were obviously impressed, and after the tournament they looked to the MLS to be able to see more soccer games.

The women's U.S. national team added to the sport's popularity when they won the gold medal at the 1996 Olympics in Atlanta, the first ever women's World Cup in 1998, and the silver medal at the 2000 Olympics in Sydney. Latino fans have also contributed to the sport's success. Since soccer is so popular in Latin America, many Latin Americans who move to the United States continue to support the game here. Also, Latino players have become more sought after by the MLS for their experience and expertise in the sport. This is a win-win situation for the league, because the more Latino players there are in the MLS, the more Latino fans will go out to support the games. "Latino fans have really supported the teams, especially in New York, Los Angeles, and Miami," confirms Llamosa. In these cities, al-most half the spectators are Latino.

"It used to be when you drove around a city, you would see kids playing football or baseball. Now I see kids playing soccer," says Llamosa. At the games in Washington, D.C., when Llamosa played for D.C. United, he remembers the stands being fairly full. "We would get about 30,000 fans at each game, which was pretty good for a sport that just got started a couple years ago in this country," he adds.

According to Llamosa, who became a U.S. citizen in 1998, being a member of the U.S. national senior team has been the highlight of his career. One of his most memorable moments came in 2000 when he had to play a game for the national squad against the national team from Colombia, his native country. Captain of the national team for the day, Llamosa says he felt especially proud of himself and his teammates. Although the U.S. lost by a score of 1-0, Llamosa says, "We played pretty good."

The second favorite moment of his career also took place in 2000, when he again was called to play with the national team against the national team from Guatemala. On this day, however, he was also scheduled to play on his MLS team, D.C. United. Llamosa played both games and became the only American player to play for both teams in the same day. "I really appreciate playing on the U.S. national team; it's one of the high points of my career," he says. "I really feel like I'm part of something important when I'm on this team."

He has a good chance of playing on the U.S. national team in the 2002 World Cup, which will take place in Japan and South Korea. Llamosa may not get to play in the 2004 Summer Olympics in Athens, Greece, however. Currently, the age limit for most of the soccer players chosen to compete in the Olympics is 23 years old. Three players from the senior team (over 23) will be chosen, and Llamosa hopes to be one of them.

Llamosa loves everything about the game, and that includes practicing. On an average workday Llamosa gets up at 8:00 A.M. and goes directly to the team gym to begin training. He spends two hours practicing with the team, and then goes home for a few hours. Three days a week, he returns to the gym to do weight training and exercises. His easiest day is Monday because he only trains in the mornings and is off the rest of the day.

Llamosa has focused on becoming a good defender and has been recognized by sports journalists and his coaches for it. According to his former D.C. United coach Bruce Arena, "[Carlos] is a pure defender. He is excellent anticipating plays, positioning himself properly, getting in on tackles." Another former coach from D.C. United, Thomas Rongen, agrees. "Carlos is a very strong tackler and has great positioning. He rarely makes mistakes and reads the game very well. He's one of the best man markers in MLS."

Llamosa says the most important job of the defender is to stay alert. In soccer, defenders remain on their side of the field while the offense is pushing the ball forward onto the opposing team's side of the field. Because the ball can change possession, and thereby direction, very quickly, defenders need to stay behind to defend their side of the field (although they have been known to score occasionally). According to Llamosa, it's when the ball is on the opposite side of the field that defenders can get distracted and become vulnerable to a sudden play or kick that sends the ball back in their direction. "Concentration is important," he explains. "You have to be ready, even when the ball is away from you. In a matter of seconds a defender can lose the ball and endanger his position. You have to play the whole ninety minutes of the game in order to be a good defender."

Being in good shape is essential for a soccer player. The soccer field is bigger than a football field, measuring 110 feet long by 75 feet wide, and each soccer period (there are two in a game) is 45 minutes long. The season lasts for six to seven months, and players will compete in 40 games or more if the team makes it to the playoffs. For young people who may consider a career in soccer, Llamosa stresses that discipline is very important. "If you have good discipline, you will be a good player." Part of being a disciplined player is not only practicing, but playing with enthusiasm. Even though it looks like soccer players have to run a lot on the field, Llamosa says that if a player is smart, he or she won't have to waste a lot of energy running. "If you practice, you don't have to work so hard [on the field]," he says.

A father of two young sons— Esteban who is seven and Carlos Andres who is three—Llamosa also feels strongly about being a role model. He knows that young kids, especially Latinos, may look up to him and watch how he acts, on and off the playing field. With this in mind, he always takes the time to sign autographs and talk to the fans. "I see players who have big names but don't take the time with the fans. That's not the way [the fans] should be treated," he says.

For Llamosa, the most important attribute of a professional athlete is a good personality. "This is a sport where you meet a lot of people from around the world. You have to treat all these people equally," he says. "As a professional athlete, you have to be ready for autographs, pictures, everything, and you have to be ready for them everywhere, in the street, in a restaurant, in a mall, in your house. You have to be ready for that."

Now settled in Miami with his wife, Marion, and their two boys, Llamosa looks forward to his career with the Fusion. He's experienced good and bad times since his move to the United States from Colombia, but with soccer back as a major part of his life, the future looks pretty bright.

John Ruiz

Boxer

Records are broken every day in the world of sports, but the athlete who is the first to do something is especially celebrated. Being the first guarantees that an athlete will never be forgotten. For John Ruiz, that day came on March 4, 2001, when he beat Evander Holyfield in the World Boxing Association (WBA) match and became the first Latino heavyweight to win the title of heavyweight champion of the world. "That's the greatest, personally, to be the first in history," Ruiz says.

Born January 4, 1972, in Methuen, Massachusetts, a Boston suburb, Ruiz and his two brothers and one sister would move to Puerto Rico in 1974 with their parents, Bienvenido Ruiz and Gladys Martinez. They lived there until 1978. His parents separated that year, which prompted his mother to move the family back to Boston and settle in a neighborhood called Chelsea. His mother is still alive, but his biological father has passed away.

In Boston, Gladys met a man who suggested that she get the boys boxing lessons. A former boxer himself, the man thought boxing would not only provide good exercise, it would also teach John and his brothers important skills for defending themselves, since Chelsea was considered a rough neighborhood. He took the boys to the gym to see if they liked the sport. While his brothers decided that they'd rather not, John was hooked. "I had tried other sports, but I've loved boxing ever since that first day. I kept it up from then on," Ruiz says.

What appealed to him early on, he says, was how things changed once he stepped into the ring. Other boxers have said the same thing. They describe how once inside the ring they focus immediately on their opponent and everything else around them disappears. They don't hear the crowd or see the cameras flashing. All the boxers see is the face of their opponent. "When you step into the ring, it's a one-on-one situation," explains Ruiz. "You have to figure out who's the best. [You] have to think about fighting and winning each round. For me, winning is the only thing, because I'm looking out for my family."

Heavyweights like Mike Tyson or Evander Holyfield were given a lot of press once they began fighting professionally. Ruiz, however, seemed to emerge from nowhere. He hadn't received the kind of media attention that these boxers received before they became heavyweight champs. Part of that may be due to Ruiz's reputation or nickname, Quiet Man. But Ruiz contends that he has been working consistently to achieve his goal of becoming heavyweight champ since those first moments in a gym. "I've been working hard. I didn't avoid any fight, I took every fight even if sometimes they were just locals," he says. Little by little, he built up his fight record to 35 wins and four defeats, which got him noticed by boxing promoters who were looking for an opponent for Holyfield.

Actually, this was not the first meeting for the two boxers. One of Ruiz's defeats came at the hands of Holyfield when they met for the first time August 12, 2000. Although Holyfield was declared the victor, many reporters who saw the fight claimed that Ruiz should have won. In the rematch, Ruiz stood his ground against the champion and even knocked him down in the 11th round (there are 12 rounds in a championship boxing match).

"It was an ugly fight," wrote Tim Dahlberg of the Associated Press, "filled with fouls and clinches, and Ruiz's bloodied and puffy face looked even worse. But he triumphed in a war against the fighter who calls himself a warrior. He took control of a close fight with a huge right hand early in the eleventh round that put Holyfield down for one of the few times in his career." Ruiz's response after the fight was "It's a joy and an honor. I feel speechless." His record is now 36–4 with 27 knockouts.

There have been many Latino boxing champions but never in the heavyweight class. Boxing is broken down by a boxer's weight. The different weight classes—lightweight, welterweight, heavyweight, etc.—correspond to a weight range. For amateur heavyweights, the range is 215–250 pounds. Professional heavyweights weigh 191 pounds or more (unlimited). At a height of six feet, two inches, Ruiz weighs in at 230 pounds.

Although he loves the sport of boxing, Ruiz admits that there are some drawbacks. His biggest concern is that boxers can really be hurt in the ring, especially if they're not sufficiently trained. "I've seen people die in that ring," he admits. He would like to see more structure put into the sport that would include rules requiring a boxer to box as an amateur for a minimum number of years before being allowed to box as a professional. "This way, a boxer would have experience and training before stepping into a professional fight," he explains.

Ideally, Ruiz would like to see boxing become a collegiate sport. Currently, boxers begin their careers in local gyms run privately or through city programs. Along the way, if they show some talent, they may find a coach to help them and begin boxing as an amateur in the Golden Gloves, one of the largest amateur boxing programs, or USA Boxing, which represents the boxing federation for the U.S. Olympic team. Since boxing takes place outside a school setting, many times a boxer sacrifices an education in order to pursue the sport. "I'd like to see boxing become a collegiate sport, the way it used to be," enthuses Ruiz. "That way a boxer would not only get important training at an amateur level, he could also get a college education by winning a sports scholarship."

Ruiz admits that he still loves the sport of boxing, and it's because of his feelings that he wants to see it improved. Requiring more training from amateurs and giving the sport more structure by making it a collegiate sport would help give meaning to the word *professional* when it relates to boxing. "I say I'm a professional fighter, but it doesn't mean that much because anyone can box and be a professional fighter. Setting up rules to spend more time as an amateur will make sure fighters really know how to box, which is the difference between succeeding in boxing or just coming off the streets and stepping into a ring," Ruiz asserts. "This will also benefit the fans, who will get to see better fights, and better fights will improve the boxing world. Boxing today is at a standstill. We're still boxing like we did back in the day. We need to bring it into the future."

Finally, Ruiz has one more concern. The career for a boxer is usually not very long. For many it lasts 10 to 12 years, if they're not injured too badly. If a boxer is successful, he can earn a lot of money during that time, but if he's not careful, at the end of his career he can find himself broke and with few options for making a living. As a boxer ages, there are also additional health concerns that come up. Ruiz would like to see some kind of retirement fund established for former boxers so that when their careers are over, they will still have some means of support. "Boxing is a great sport and it makes a lot of money for a lot of people, but it seems to me like the fighters are the ones who get left behind. I look at ex-boxers today, many are broke and have no means of support. It's time we change that and take care of the ones who sacrificed to keep this sport alive," he asserts.

Raising the standards in the world of professional boxing will also help increase the pay range for all boxers, not just the ones who become champions. Currently, non-amateur fighters who have not trained as Olympic athletes can earn between $100 and $500 per fight. As a fighter's record improves, he can eventually earn more. Ruiz earned $1 million for the 2000 fight and will earn more for his next fight with Holyfield.

Boxing is seen as an inner-city sport. Many times the sport is introduced into a community as a means of providing an after-school activity to keep kids out of trouble. Because of this, boxing is one of the sports that is considered very open to Latinos. That has been a good and bad thing for the sport, says Ruiz. "Boxing is one of the few sports where you don't have to know how to box but can still become a professional fighter. Anyone who has a pulse can box." That doesn't mean that they'll box successfully, he adds, and although he believes boxing has brought him tremendous opportunities and is a very open sport for Latinos, the changes he lists would improve the sport for everyone.

Some sports require quickness and agility, while others may favor power and strength. According to Ruiz, a boxer needs all of these abilities and more to be successful. Agility and speed are required for good footwork and hand speed. Power and strength will help a boxer take punches as well as throw them effectively. The most important thing for a boxer to have before getting into the ring, however, is skill and knowledge of boxing. "If you're not close to knowing what you're doing in that ring, anything can happen. You will get hit, and hit, and hit, and you may even end up dying," he stresses.

Growing up in Boston, Ruiz admits that he never watched boxing on television or in person, so he was unfamiliar with any famous champions. "I usually went to the gym or straight home after school. I didn't have time to watch boxing," he says. He did have a role model growing up, and that was his mother, who, as a single parent, worked to support the family. "My mom worked so hard to make sure we had food on the table and clothes on our backs. She gave us the attitude to have strength and keep going no matter what."

On an average day during his prefight training, Ruiz will get up at 8:00 A.M. and run for about an hour and a half. In the afternoon, he will go to the gym and focus on weight training for a few hours. He'll go home and take a break, to eat and rest, and then go back to the gym and spar (practice boxing) with another boxer for an hour.

He wants his children to make their own decisions about whether or not they will become boxers. He makes a point of not talking about boxing while he's at home so as not to influence them. He and his wife, Sahara, have a daughter, Jocelyn, who's eight years old, and a son, Johnny, who is eleven.

One of his favorite memories is of when he was eight years old. Ruiz and his family—Gladys, brothers Robert and Edward, and sister Jackie (they're named after the Kennedys)—lived in a housing project in Chelsea. Housing projects were built by the government to provide affordable housing for poor people. Across the street from the project was a square patch of grass. Ruiz says that his stepfather, Junior Rivera, would set up a pretend ring in the square and invite the neighborhood kids to come and spar with them for a couple of rounds. It impressed Ruiz, who says, "I thought that was kinda awesome for him to do that."

Although the family was aware of their daily struggles, Ruiz says he never stopped dreaming and he thinks that has helped him. Children should never stop hoping or dreaming, he says, so that when they get older, they can put the effort into making that dream come true. "When it does," he adds, "it's the most wonderful feeling. It's a feeling that's hard to explain, it's wonderful."

"Sports saved me from going in a negative direction. Where I grew up, everything was gangs, drugs, and alcohol. Boxing and school saved me. It taught me to know the difference between what's right and wrong. It's important for kids to spend time wisely and do something positive. Always follow your dream. It doesn't have to be sports, just something that will make you happy because you know you're doing something good."

Brenda Villa

Water Polo Player

Water polo is a pretty tough sport. Players have to be able to tread water or swim the length of a pool while trying to keep control of a ball that's only too happy to float, bounce, and skid along the surface of the water. To score, players have to take the ball in one hand, lift themselves above the outstretched and waving arms of the defender, and throw the ball past the goaltender and into the net. At eight years old, Brenda Villa took the sport on. Eventually she would play on the boy's team of her junior high school and then on the U.S. Olympic team.

"My older brother [Edgar] started playing water polo before I did. Growing up, I would follow him everywhere and wanted to do everything he did. I bugged my mom about joining a water polo team. Eventually she gave in," recounts Villa. She joined the polo team run by the city of Commerce, California, where she was born on April 18, 1980, and where she grew up. Villa and her brother first took swimming lessons before moving on to water polo. "My mom didn't want us to be afraid of the water," she says. Her parents, Ines and Rosario Villa, emigrated to the United States from Mexico.

Brenda Villa pursued the sport in school, and that's how she eventually played with her brother Edgar on the junior high team. "I was fifteen, and since there wasn't a girls' team they allowed me to play with the boys. That was a great experience, not only playing with my brother but with boys. I think it helps me today because I had to learn to be really quick, since the boys were stronger and bigger than I was," she offers. Villa's younger brother, Uriel, also plays water polo.

It's not considered a big team sport like baseball or basketball, but water polo did change Villa's life in many ways. She earned an athletic scholarship to Stanford University through the sport, and she has traveled around the world as a member of the U.S. Olympic team. She remembers watching the Olympics as a little girl and even dreaming of becoming an Olympic athlete. "I remember thinking I would be a gymnast or a swimmer at first," she says.

Even if she had thought of it, it would have been impossible for Villa to be an Olympic water polo player at the time. Although men's water polo had been an Olympic event since 1900, it wasn't until the Sydney games in 2000 that a women's water polo event was included in the Olympics. "Naturally, when I started playing water polo, I gave up an Olympic dream. I was thrilled when in 1998 it was announced that women's water polo would be included in Sydney," she says.

To become an Olympian today in water polo, Villa explains, the natural path is to attend sports clinics, usually during the summer, put on by USA Water Polo. These clinics also provide funds for USA Water Polo, which they use to help pay expenses for members of the national team who have to attend international tournaments throughout the year.

At these clinics, young athletes are taught the fundamentals of the sport. Villa admits that she didn't have the opportunity to attend any clinics, but she was able to succeed because of the nature of the sport. Since water polo is a smaller sport, she was able to train through her local clubs and, later, in school. "Because it's so small, the chances are pretty good that you'll be seen at a tournament by a national team coach," Villa asserts. She was picked for the U.S. Olympic team when she was just 16. "I've traveled everywhere with water polo, which has been amazing," she says. "It's given me a lot of opportunities that maybe one of the other big team sports wouldn't have."

The next Summer Olympics will take place in 2004 in Athens, Greece. Villa, who will be 24 years old by then, hopes to attend. Her experience as an Olympian is one of the high points of her life. She can still remember being amazed by all the cultures and countries that came together for this one event. "I remember sitting in the cafeteria with all the other athletes and hearing all these different languages flowing from every corner of the room. I wished I could speak them all so that I could communicate with everyone," she asserts.

At the 2000 Olympics, Team USA performed much better than expected, winning the silver medal in women's water polo. Some sportswriters predicted that the women's team would win a bronze medal, but none expected them to make it to a gold-medal match. Still, Villa says that her Olympic experience went beyond winning a medal. She believes: "Winning a medal isn't really what the Olympics is about. It's about all the hard work you put in to get there and represent your country. Not everyone will win a gold medal. In my experience, I met so many people and formed so many friendships from two years of training and trying to qualify. I just think there's more to it than, like, medals."

Although she's passionate about water polo, there is one disadvantage to playing a smaller team sport, Villa says, and that's money. "There's never enough money for a small sport," she concedes. Because most water polo players come from California, where swimming can be done year round, getting national sponsors to support the sport is difficult. As a professional player, there are even fewer opportunities. Male players can find work on international leagues, but for women, the pay on these leagues is not worth the sacrifice of leaving home and living abroad. While playing for the national team, Villa says other players were approached by coaches from professional international teams to play for them. The salary they offered, however, was not tempting. "I would have had to give up my college career, and it wouldn't have been worth it," she relates.

As a college athlete, Villa is also restricted as to the amount of money she can earn and the sources from which the money can come. Although the USOC relaxed its rules about allowing only amateur athletes to compete, Villa has to follow the rules of the National Collegiate Athletics Association (NCAA), which governs collegiate sports. The NCAA rules require that an athlete maintain an amateur status, which means they cannot receive payment or charge fees for being an athlete. Because of this rule, Villa had to return the money she received from the USOC after winning the silver medal in Sydney. "Half the players were able to keep the check and the other half had to decline it," she explains.

In order to support herself, Villa may have to look for a "day job," something she can do in her spare time that will pay her a little money, like working at a restaurant or in an office. She has also considered coaching water polo youth leagues. For Villa, the situation would be ideal, because as a water polo coach she would still be involved in the sport, have access to the pool, and could work out whenever she needed to.

A political science major at Stanford, Villa realizes that after she graduates she will have to find a way of making a living, especially if she hopes to continue playing on the national team. Coaching appears to be her best option. One of her teammates is a coach at the University of California at Los Angeles (UCLA). Other teammates have found work as assistant coaches at junior colleges. "I think it would be fun to coach, especially little kids," she says. She also has other plans for her future, which may include law school. A coaching job will help her support this goal and at the same time offer personal satisfaction. "I would like to get kids at a young age and be able to have an impact on them."

For Latinos who hope to take up the sport, Villa says it's pretty open. The club she joined as a child is one of the most competitive in the city of Commerce and has a large proportion of Latino players. The team has been very successful. Villa remembers attending and winning many tournaments as a member of the team. "In my community it was very accessible, but I also grew up in an area where swimming is very popular. That may be the only limitation—swimming pools aren't as common or accessible as, say, a basketball court," she says. Four of the five most competitive water polo teams at the college level are from California universities. Stanford is in that group.

Water polo is a physically tough sport. It requires players to tread water for four periods, so obviously being a good swimmer is a key skill in order to play the game. According to the rules of the game, each period should last at least seven minutes, but because the clock is constantly stopped due to fouls or time-outs, periods last much longer. "A game will usually last forty-five minutes," says Villa. "I don't think you could have one that was exactly twenty-eight minutes long."

Villa performs in the attacker/driver position, which is an offensive role. Whether she's on her side of the pool or in a defensive position on the opponents' side, Villa remains on the periphery (boundary) of the formation. She scopes out the action and keeps her eye on any opportunity to pass the ball into a good position or try to score herself.

Some positions, however, will not play a full period because they are considered more rigorous. As Villa explains, the center-forward position is particularly difficult because it requires the player to remain in front of the goal. If she can manage to receive a pass, the center-forward is in the best position to score, but because this is the most vulnerable position for the defense, the defenders must keep the center-forward distracted. To do this she is constantly pulled, pushed, dunked, and held. If the offense loses possession of the ball, the center-forward also has to swim the farthest. For this reason, center-forwards are substituted many times in a game to rest.

Besides the physical requirements, it's also important for an athlete to be committed to the sport. As Villa demonstrates, it takes years of practice and dedication to compete on an international level. Even Villa, who had experience and was in great shape, was severely tested by the training she was required to do after joining the national team. "Training for Sydney was horrible," she recalls.

The hardest days took place three times a week when the players had to do weight training. The players began the day at 7:30 A.M. and ran about a mile to the gym, where they would work out with weights. After weight training they would run back to the pool, where they would do circuit training. This involved exercises such as jumping rope, running in place, throwing a medicine ball, or running up and down the stadium stairs. After that they did swimming conditioning. "Half the day would be over, and we still hadn't been in the pool and played any water polo," says Villa.

Following the conditioning, the players would be given a three-hour break to eat and rest a little. When they returned they'd be put through an intense water polo workout, which included scrimmaging (playing a practice game), shooting drills, and constant movement. "By the end of the day, you're dead," says Villa. "I went to bed by eight-thirty or nine at night." Although the training on the Stanford team is a little less difficult, Villa mentions that she still has to juggle classes and schoolwork with her athletic commitments.

Besides being a good swimmer and being committed to the sport, having a competitive spirit also helps an athlete. The physical nature of the sport probably helps grow a competitive nature as well, Villa proposes. At the Olympics, she and her fellow teammates were extremely competitive, to the point where she says it got ridiculous. Everything they did, someone had to be the fastest or the first. "It got to the point where we had to laugh and ask, 'Why are we competing over this?'" In the pool, however, a strong desire to win always helps.

She believes that getting into a pool and playing water polo early in life has been a key to her success. Even though she wasn't as skilled then as she is now, she had the chance to watch older, more skilled players, which she believes inspired her. "I don't have one player I admired, there were several. I remember at age eight, sitting beside the pool, I couldn't even throw the ball then, but I watched the older players practice. Eventually I played with boys, too, until I got into college. That was a huge part of my success," she asserts.

Although she has enjoyed her athletic career, Villa advises kids to focus on their education first. Second, they should remember that there are lots of other sports available beyond the main team sports and to take the time to find a sport they like. She chose a smaller sport, but she has no regrets. "I've been able to travel and get a college scholarship through water polo. There are plenty of opportunities out there in the smaller sports. Coaches get paid pretty well. You could also become an athletic director. Kids and parents shouldn't get stuck on big-time sports, because the smaller sports can offer just as much, or probably even more."

Playing a sport she loves, regardless of its popularity or ability to pay a big salary, has proved to be the right choice for Villa. And whether she becomes a water polo coach or a lawyer, she'll always be an Olympian.

Brenda Villa surveys the defense and looks for a scoring opportunity.

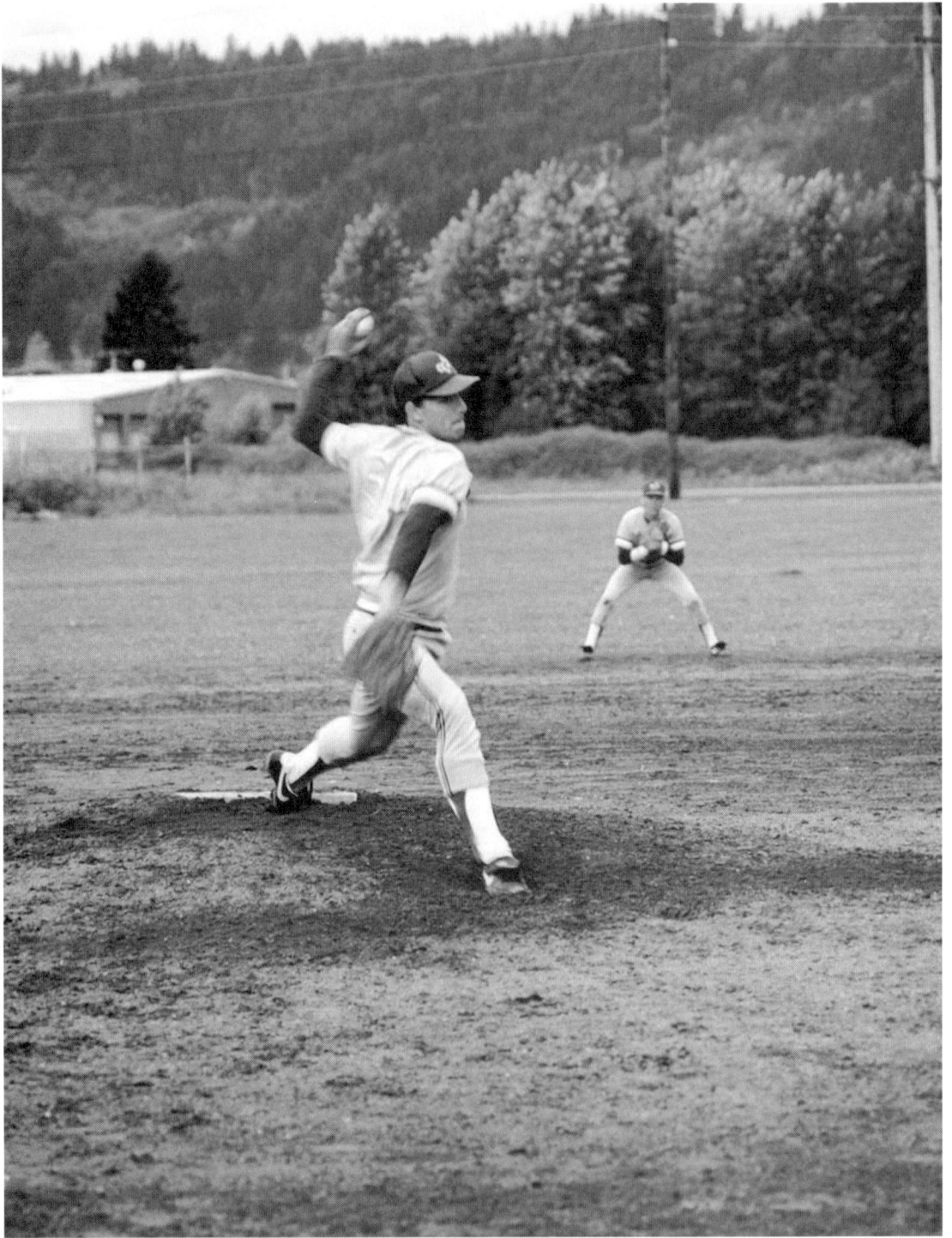

PART
3

Resources

Books   84

Internet Sources   89

Master Index to Careers   90

Master Index to People Profiled   92

Index to this book   96

Books

Abramson, Hilary S. *The Princeton Review Student Athlete's Guide to College.* New York: Random House, Inc., 1999.

Barber, Mike. *Athletic Scholarships.* Hurricane, WY: Baca Sports Books, 1997.

Caven, Todd P., and Penny Hastings. *How to Win a Sports Scholarship.* Los Angeles: First Base Sports, Inc., 1999.

Chambers, Dave. *Coaching: Winning Strategies for Every Level of Play.* Buffalo, NY: Firefly Books, 1977.

Clarkson, Michael. *Competitive Fire: Insights to Developing the Warrior Mentality of Sports Champions.* Champaign, IL: Human Kinetics, 1999.

Devenzio, Dick. *Smart Moves: How to Succeed in School, Sports, Career, and Life.* Amherst, NY: Prometheus Books, 1989.

Ferguson Staff. *Careers in Sports.* Second Edition. Chicago: Ferguson Publishing, 1999.

———. *Preparing for a Career in Sports (What Can I Do Now).* Chicago: Ferguson Publishing, 1998.

Field, Shelly. *Career Opportunities in the Sports Industry.* Second Edition. New York: Facts on File, 1999.

Fischer, David. *The 50 Coolest Jobs in Sports: Who's Got Them, What They Do, and How You Can Get One.* New York: Macmillian, 1997.

Flores, Tom, and Bob O'Conner. *Coaching Football.* Lincolnwood, IL: Masters Press, 1993.

———. *Youth League Football: Coaching and Playing.* Lincolnwood, IL: Masters Press, 1993.

Grunska, Jerry. *Successful Sports Officiating.* Champaign, IL: Human Kinetics, 1999.

Heitzmann, William Ray. *Careers for Sports Nuts and Other Athletic Types.* Lincolnwood, IL: VGM Career Horizons, 1993.

Mazzoni, Wayne. *Athletic Recruiting and Scholarship Guide.* New York: Mazz Marketing, 1998.

The Olympic Games: Athens 1896–Sidney 2000. London: Dorling Kindersley Publishing, Inc., 1998.

Pasternack, Ceel, and Linda Thornbur. *Cool Careers for Girls in Sports (Cool Careers for Girls in Sports Series).* Manassas, VA: Impact Publications, 1999.

Ratermann, Dale. *How to Get a Job in Sports.* Minneapolis: Econo-Clad Books, 1999.

Roberts, Robin. *Careers for Women Who Love Sports (Get in the Game! With Robin Roberts).* Brookfield, CT: Millbrook Press, 2000.

Sandol, Joli, and Toby Winans, editors. *Whatever It Takes: Women on Women in Sports.* New York: Farrar, Straus and Giroux, 1999.

Savage, Jeff. *A Career in Professional Sports (Getting Ready).* Mankato, MN: Capstone Press, 1996.

Schaap, Dick, editor. *The Best American Sports Writing 2000.* Boston: Houghton Mifflin Company, 2000.

Shenk, Ellen. *Outdoor Careers: Exploring Occupations in Outdoor Fields.* Second Edition. Mechanicsburg, PA: Stackpole Books, 2000.

Walker, Ron, editor. *Peterson's Sports Scholarships and College Athletic Programs.* Fourth Edition. Princeton, NJ: Thompson Learning, 1999.

Finding a Job

General

National Academy of Sports (NAS), 220 East 63rd Street, New York, NY 10021. 212-838-2980.

National Collegiate Athletic Association (NCAA), 700 West Washington Street, P.O. Box 6222, Indianapolis, IN 46206-6222. 317-917-6222. www.ncaa.com

United States Olympic Committee (USOC), One Olympic Plaza, Colorado Springs, CO 80909-5746. 719-632-5551. www.usolympicteam.com

United States Olympic Education Center, c/o Northern Michigan University, Marquette, MI 49855-5300. 906-227-2888.

Individual Sports

American Horse Shows Association, 4047 Ironworks Parkway, Lexington, KY 40511. 606-258-2472. www.asha.org

Golden Gloves Association of America (GGAA), 2000 South Colorado Boulevard, Tower 1, Suite 11000, Denver, CO 80222. 303-584-9889. www.goldengloves.org

Harness Horse Youth Foundation (HHYF), 14950 Greyhount Court, Suite 210, Carmel, IN 46032. 317-848-5132. www.hhyf.org

Ladies Professional Golf Association of America (LPGA), 100 International Golf Drive, Daytona Beach, Florida 32124-1092. 386-274-6200. www.lpga.com

Professional Golfers Association of America (PGA), 100 Avenue of The Champions, Box 109601, Palm Beach Gardens, FL 33410-9601. 561-624-8400. www.pga.com

United States Diving, Inc., Pan American Plaza, Suite 430, 201 South Capitol Avenue, Indianapolis, IN 46225. 317-237-5252. www.usdiving.org

United States Judo Association (USJA), 21 North Union Boulevard, Colorado Springs, CO 80909. 719-633-7750. www.csprings.com/usja/

United States Tennis Association (USTA), 70 West Red Oak Lane, White Plains, NY 10604. 800-990-8782. www.usta.com

USA Boxing, One Olympic Plaza, Colorado Springs, CO 80909-5776. 719-578-4506. www.usaboxing.org

USA Cycling, Inc., One Olympic Plaza, Colorado Springs, CO 80909-5775. 719-578-4581. www.usacycling.org

USA Gymnastics, Pan American Plaza, Suite 300, 201 South Capitol Avenue, Indianapolis, IN 46225. 317-237-5050. www.usa-gymnastics.org

USA Swimming, One Olympic Plaza, Colorado Springs, CO 80909-5770. 719-578-4578. www.usswim.org

USA Weightlifting, One Olympic Plaza, Colorado Springs, CO 80909-5764. 719-578-4508. www.usaweightlifting.org

U.S. Equestrian Team (USET), Pottersville Road, P.O. Box 355, Gladstone, NJ 07934. 908-234-1251. www.uset.com

U.S. Ski and Snowboard Association, Box 100, 1500 Kearns Boulevard, Park City, UT 84060-0100. 435-649-9090. www.usskiteam.com

U.S. Taekwondo Union, One Olympic Plaza, Suite 104C, Colorado Springs, CO 80909-5792. 719-578-4632. www.ustu.com

Women's International Boxing Federation (WIBF), Global Boxing Union (GBU), P.O. Box 398123, Miami Beach, FL 33239. 305-531-0380. www.wibf.org

World Boxing Federation (WBF), P.O. Box 3966, Bristol, TN 53762. 615-764-1161. www.worldboxingfed.com

Team Sports

Amateur Softball Association of America (ASA), 2801 N.E. 50th Street, Oklahoma City, OK 73111. 405-424-5266. www.softball.org

American Legion Baseball (ALB), P.O. Box 1055, Indianapolis, IN 46206. 317-630-1213. www.legion.org/baseball/home.htm

American Youth Soccer Organization (AYSO), 8942 Carson Street, Culver City, CA 90232. 310-636-6621. www.soccer.org

Little League Baseball (LLB), 539 Route 15 Highway, P.O. Box 3485, South Williamsport, PA 17702. 570-326-1921. www.littleleague.org

Major League Baseball, 245 Park Ave., New York, NY 10167; 212-931-7800. www.mlb.com

Major League Soccer, 110 East 42nd Street, Tenth Floor, New York, NY 10017. 212-687-1400. www.mls.com

National Association for Stock Car Auto Racing (NASCAR), P.O. Box 2875, 1801 Volosia Avenue, Daytona Beach, FL 32015. 904-253-0611. www.nascar.com

National Basketball Association (NBA), 645 Fifth Avenue, Floor 10, New York, NY 10022. 212-826-7000. www.nba.com

National Football League (NFL), 410 Park Avenue, New York, NY 10022. 212-758-1500. www.nfl.com

National Hockey League (NHL), 1800 McGill College Avenue, Suite 2600, Montreal, Quebec, Canada, H3A 3J6. 514-268-9220. www.nhl.com

Pop Warner Football (PWF), Pop Warner Little Scholars, Inc., 586 Middletown Boulevard, #C100, Langhorne, PA 19047. 215-752-2691. www.popwarner.org

United States Water Polo, 1685 West Uintah, Colorado Springs, CO 80904-2921. 719-634-0699. www.usawaterpolo.com

USA Baseball, Hi Corbett Field, 3400 East Camino Campestre, Tucson, AZ 85716. 520-327-9700. www.usabaseball.com

USA Basketball, 5465 Mark Dabling Boulevard, Colorado Springs, CO 80918-3842. 719-590-4800. www.usabasketball.com

USA Softball, 2801 N.E. 50th Street, Oklahoma City, OK 73111-7203. 405-424-5266. www.softball.org

Women's National Basketball Association (WNBA), Olympic Tower, 645 Fifth Avenue, New York, NY 10022. 212-688-9622. www.wnba.com

Women's Professional Softball League, 90 Madison Street, Suite 200, Denver, CO 80203. 303-316-7800. www.prosoftball.com

Women's United Soccer Association (WUSA), 1120 Avenue of the Americas, 6th Floor, New York, NY 10036-6700. 212-869-8558. www.wusa.com

Officiating

Academy of Professional Umpiring, 12741 Research Boulevard, Suite 401, Austin, TX 78759. 512-335-5959. www.umpireacademy.com

International Association of Approved Basketball Officials (IAABO), 12321 Middlebrook Road, P.O. Box 1300, Germantown, MD 20875-1300. 301-601-8013. www.iaabo.org

National Association of Sports Officials (NASO), 2017 Lathrop Avenue, Racine, WI 53405. 262-632-5448. www.naso.org

Off the Field

American Sportscasters Association (ASA), 225 Broadway, Suite 2030, New York, NY 10007. 212-227-8080. www.americansportscasters.com

The Center for the Study of Sport in Society, 360 Huntington Avenue, Suite 161 CP, Boston, MA 02115-5000. 617-373-4025. www.sportinsociety.org

National Athletic Trainer's Association, 2952 Stemmons Freeway, Dallas, Texas 75247-6916. 800-879-6282. www.nata.org

Internet Sources

Jobs

Breakaway Brokers:
www.hockeyhole.com

CoachFinder:
www.coachfinder.com

Game Face, Inc.:
www.gamefaceinc.com

Independent Scouting Bureau:
www.inscouting.com/
indexn.htm

National Athletic Trainers'
Association: www.nata.org

Sports.com: www.sports.com

Sports Employment:
www.careersearchinc.com

Sports Fans of America
Association:
www.sportsfansofamerica.com

Sports Jobs for Women:
www.sportsjobsforwomen.com

SportsWorkers.com:
www.sportsworkers.com

Women In Sports Careers
Foundation:
www.womensportsjobs.com

Scholarships

American Legion Baseball:
www.legion.org/baseball/
home.htm

Athletes Bound for College:
www.athletesboundforcollege.com

College Recruiting.com:
www.collegerecruiting.com

College Sports Recruiting:
www.collegesportsrecruiter.com

Football Prospects College Sports
Scholarships and Athletic
Recruiting:
www.footballprospects.com

Free Sports Scholarships:
angelfire.com/ns/scholarship/
sports.htm

The Sports Recruiter:
www.thesportsrecruiter.com

Sports Recruits:
www.angelfire.com/al/
sportsrecruits

USA Tennis Foundation:
www.usta.com/
usatennisfoundation/
index.html

U.S. Sports Scholarships:
www.ussportsscholarships.com

Youth Athletics News:
www.usatf.org/assoc/mid-
atlantic/youthn.htm

Youth Service League:
www.youthservice.org

Master Index to Careers

· ·

actor/actress, En
acupuncturist, SM
administrative assistant, CS, Ed
advertising copywriter, En
advertising salesperson, PC
agent, En, Sp, MI
agriculturalist, SM
alternative medical practitioner, SM
ambassador, LP
animator, En
archaeologist, SM
art director, PC
associate director, nonprofit organization, CS
astronomer, SM
athlete, professional, Sp
athletic director, Sp
athletic trainer, Sp
attorney *see* lawyer
bailiff, LP
baseball umpire, Sp
biologist, SM
board member, CS
broadcast engineer, PC
broadcaster *see also* journalist, CS
bus driver, Ed
business owner, LE
casting director, En
chemist, SM
chief executive officer/executive director/
    president, CS, LE
chiropractor, SM
choreographer, En
cinematographer (director of photography), En
city administrator, LP
classified worker, Ed
coach/manager, Ed, Sp
columnist, PC
comedian, En
comedy writer, En
communications/media relations/public
    relations officer, CS
community affairs director (television), En

composer, En, MI
computer engineer, Tc
computer programmer, Tc
computer technician, Tc
conductor, MI
copyeditor, PC
copywriter, PC
costume designer (theater/television/film), En
court reporter, LP
crime prevention specialist, LP
criminal defense lawyer, LP
critic/reviewer, En, MI
data base manager, Tc
data entry clerk, Tc
data processing technician, Tc
dental hygienist, SM
dentist, SM
director (feature films or television), En
disc jockey/radio announcer, PC, MI
editor, PC
engineer, SM
engineering technician, SM
equipment manager, Sp
FBI agent, LP
film editor, En
fingerprint expert, LP
football referee, Sp
foreign service officer, LP
forester, SM
founder, CS, LE
fund-raiser for nonprofit organization, CS
general manager (station manager), PC
geologist, SM
government relations officer, LP
grant writer, CS
graphic designer, PC, Tc
graphics programmer, Tc
guidance counselor, Ed
home health care worker, CS
human rights worker, LP
immigration and customs officer, LP
instructional assistant, Ed

KEY
CS—Community Service
Ed—Education
En—Entertainment
LE—Latino Entrepreneurs
LP—Law and Politics

MI—Music Industry
PC—Publishing and Communications
SM—Science and Medicine
Sp—Sports
Tc—Technology

Instrumental musician, MI
journalist, CS, En, LP, PC, Sp, MI
judge, LP
justice of the peace, LP
juvenile detention officer, LP
labor representative (organizer, regional
    director), CS
laboratory technician, SM
lawyer (attorney, paralegal), CS, En, LP, Sp
    legal secretary, LP
librarian, Ed
lighting designer (theater), En
makeup artist (theater/television/film), En
manufacturer's representative, Sp
marketing director, Sp
medical doctor, CS, SM
medical scientist, SM
meteorologist/weather forecaster, PC, SM
music librarian, MI
news director, PC
news writer (radio), PC
notary public, LP
nurse, CS, SM
nutritionist, SM
optometrist, SM
paramedic, emergency medical technician
    (EMT), SM
parole officer, LP
personal trainer, Sp
pharmacist, SM
photographer or camera operator, PC
physical therapist, SM
physician, SM
physicist, SM
playwright, En
podiatrist, SM
police officer, LP
political lobbyist, LP
political strategist, LP
politician, LP
press agent, En
principal, Ed
probation officer, LP
producer, En, MI
professional scout, Sp
professor, college or university, Ed
program director, PC
promoter, music and events, MI
proofreader, PC
psychiatrist, SM
psychologist, Ed, SM
public relations director, En, PC, Sp
publicist, Sp
publicity director, PC
publisher, PC

radio producer, PC
recording engineer, MI
recording technician, MI
representative (Congress), LP
retail manager or clerk, MI
sales representative (books), PC
scenic designer (theater), En
science technician, SM
screenwriter, En
senator, LP
set designer (theater/television/film/video),
    En
singer, MI
sound editor, En
sound technician, MI
sports reporter/sportscaster, PC, Sp
stage director, En
stage manager, En
superintendent (school), Ed
systems analyst, Tc
teacher, Ed
    technical support specialist, Tc
technical writer, PC
television news anchor, PC
tour publicist, En
tuner, musical instruments, MI
translator/interpreter, LP
treaty negotiator, LP
veterinarian, SM
victim advocate, LP
Web master, Tc
writer, book, PC
youth coordinator, CS

Master Index to People Profiled

• •

Acosta, Angela, Media Relations, Community Relations Director , CS

Acrivos, Juana Vivó, Professor of Chemistry, SM

Ahmed, Ada Diaz, founder and president of failed Latina Web site, Tc

Alonso, José Jr., Physicist, SM

Alvarado, Linda, Baseball Team Owner, Sp

Alvarez, Joe, Police Officer, Supervisor of Crime Stoppers, LP

Anaya, Rudolfo, Writer , PC

Ancira, Ernesto, Car Dealer, LE

Arellano, Jairo, Assistant Principal, Ed

Baca, Bettie, Senior Executive Service Candidate, LP

Baca, James, Mayor, LP

Barbosa, Pedro, Entomologist, SM

Belli, Gioconda, Writer, PC

Benitez, John "Jellybean," disc jockey, recording artist, record producer, MI

Bezos, Jeff, founder and CEO of on-line store, Tc

Brown, Sarita, Educational Programs Administrator, Ed

Burr, Ramiro, music critic, MI

Canosa, Daniel, Conductor, Composer, MI

Cardona, Carlos, founder and senior vice president of Hispanic Web site, Tc

Carrera, Mario M., Senior Media Sales Executive, PC

Casillas, Ederlen, Codirector of nonprofit organization, CS

Centeno, Oscar, Business Owner, Trucking Company, LE

Chavez, Gabriel, Business Owner, Technology Company, LE

Cuellar, Henry, Secretary of State (Texas), LP

Davidds-Garrido, Norberto, professional football player, Sp

de la Hoya, Oscar, Professional Boxer, Sp

Del Olmo, Frank, Vice President of Professional Programs, CS

Del Toro, Benicio, Actor, En

Diaz, Freddy, graphic artist and graphic arts teacher, Tc

Diaz, Guadalupe "Aura," computer artist, Tc

Dominguez, Isabel, Geneticist, SM

Escalante, Jaime, Math Teacher, Ed, SM

Esparza, Moctesuma, Producer, En

Fernandez, Lisa, Softball Player, Sp

Flores, Tom, Football Coach, Sp

Galindo, Max, Paramedic, SM

Garcia, Abraham and Ana Corinna, Business Owners, Computer Company, LE

Garcia, Paul, Web master, Tc

Garcia, Rodolfo, Relationship Banker, LP

Gates, Ann Quiroz, computer science professor, Tc

Girón, Carlos, Sports Publicist, Sp

Gomez, Julio, founder and owner of e-commerce consulting firm, Tc

Gonzales, Enrique, project manager for a network of Web sites, Tc

Gonzales, Thomas, technology consultant, Tc

Gonzales, Victor, computer programmer, Tc

Gonzalez, Alex, Baseball Player, Sp

Guerrero, Lena, Political Lobbyist, LP

Gutiérrez, Margo, Librarian, Ed

Guzman-Macias, Estela, Special Education Teacher, Resource Specialist, Ed

Hayek, Salma Actress, En

Henley, Maria Jimenez, Stage Manager, Assistant Director, Choreographer, and Dancer, En

Hernandez, Antonia, Lawyer, President, CS

Hernandez, Fidel, Zoologist, SM

Hernandez, G. Herb, County Councilman at Large, LP

Hernandez-Castillo, Bel, Publisher, Editor-in-Chief, Dancer, and Actress, En

Herrera, Leticia, Business Owner, Cleaning Service, LE

Heumann, Judith, Assistant Secretary for Special Education, Ed

Jaime, Mental Health Technician, SM

Jimenez, James, City Administrator, LP

Kanellos, Nicolás, Book Publisher, PC

Leanos, John, Cultural Worker, Artist, LE

Leguizamo, John, Actor, Comedian, Playwright, En

Leoni, Dennis Edward, Writer, Producer, En

Llamosa, Carlos, Soccer Player, Sp

Llanes, David, Record Company owner, MI

Lopez, George, Comedian, En

Los Lobos (David Hidalgo, Conrad Lozano, Louie Perez, and Cesar Rosas), musicians, MI

Martinez, Christine, radio disc jockey, MI

Martinez, Gilbert, Chief Judge, LP

Martinez, Rueben, Bookstore Owner, PC

Martinez, Walter, Magazine Publisher, Editor, PC

Massó, Jose, Center for the Study of Sport in Society, Sp

McBride, Theresa, computer systems consultant, Tc

Melendez, Bill, Animator, Producer, En

Mendoza, Araceli, Business Owner, Beauty Salon, LE

Mendoza, Graciela Contreras, Head Start Teacher, Ed

Monterroso, Benjamin, Labor Leader, CS

Morales, Dionicio, Founder and President, CS

Morales, Hugo, Radio Station Executive Director, PC

Moran, Julio, Executive Director of nonprofit organization, CS

Moreno, Richard Blackburn, President of nonprofit organization, CS

Moreno, Rita, Actress, Performer, En

Muniz, Marc Anthony, singer, MI

Muñoz, Zoila, Opera Singer, MI

Nava, Gregory, Director, Writer, En

Nuñez, Emanuel, Agent, En

Nuñez, Tommy, Referee, Sp, CS

O'Brien, Soledad, Television News Anchor, PC

Oceguera, Frank, III, Math Teacher, Ed

Olmos, Edward James, Actor, En

Ortega, Juan C., Design Firm President, Creative Director, PC

Ortega, Theresa, Veterinarian, SM

Ortiz, Tony, Musician, MI

Penelas, Alex, Executive Mayor, LP

Perez, Lisandro, Sociology Professor, Ed

Perez, Severo, Writer, Director, Producer, En

Porras-Field, Esperanza, Business Owner, Consulting Firm, Real Estate, LE

Portillo, Wendy, process control analyst, Tc

Quintanilla, Selena, Tejano Singer, MI

Ramirez, Eddie, promoter and event organizer, MI

Ramos, Jorge, Television News Anchor, PC

Rivas, Yolanda, manager of on-line software products, Tc

Roa, Horacio, practitioner of holistic medicine, SM

Rodriguez, Douglas, Chef and Restaurant Owner, LE

Rodriguez, Eloy, Toxicologist, SM

Rojas, Nydia, singer, MI

Romo, Ricardo, University President, Ed

Ruiz, John, Boxer, Sp

Sanchez, Guillermo, Dentist, SM

Sanchez, Josephine, Associate Director, CS

Santana, Carlos, musician, MI

Santiago, Esmeralda, Writer, PC

Soto, Hilda Lorenia, e-commerce consultant, Tc

Tapia, Richard, Professor of Computational Applied Mathematics, SM

Tinjaca, Mabel, Author and Consultant in Organizational Development, LE

Tobar, Hector, National News Correspondent, PC

Trujillo, Gary, CEO of a failed Internet company, Tc

Vargas, Garrett, Software Design Engineer, PC

Vargas, Juan, Business Owner, Pinatas, LE

Villa, Brenda, Water Polo Player, Sp

Villalobos, Reynaldo, Cinematographer, Director, En

Wilkins, Ron, Probation Supervisor, LP

Yzaguirre, Raul, Executive Director of nonprofit organization, CS

Zamora, Guadalupe, Family Doctor, SM

Zamora, Jim, Crime Scene Detective, LP

Zamora, Maria, Paraprofessional Educator, Ed

Boxing is a popular sport among Latinos.

Soccer continues to grow in popularity in the United States.

Index

agent - 9, 24
Allen, Marcus - 46, 48
Alvarado, Linda - 31-35
   Colorado Rockies - 31-33
   education - 34
   family - 31, 34-35
athletic director - 21
athletic trainer - 9, 11
baseball - 8, 10, 25
   Major League Baseball (MLB) - 11-12, 31-34
   minor league - 11-12
   player - 11-12
basketball - 8-9, 25
   NBA - 14
   player - 12-13
   Women's National Basketball Association (WNBA) - 12, 28
boxer - 13, 15, 69-73
boxing - 8
bicycling - 8,
Center for the Study of Sport in Society - 25
Census 2000 - 8,
coach/managers - 9
   college/high school - 15-16
   professional - 15
Cordero, Angel - 18
Davidds-Garrido, Norberto - 17
diving - 8,
equipment manager - 16
Fernandez, Lisa - 19, 37-41
   family - 37-38, 41
   Olympics - 37-40
Flores, Tom - 43-49
   education - 43-45, 48
   family - 43-44
   Super Bowl (1981) - 43, 45-46
   Super Bowl (1984) - 43, 46
football - 8, 10
   American Football League (AFL) - 44-45
   Canadian Football League (CFL) - 16
   National Football League (NFL) - 16-17, 44-49
   player - 16
Girón, Carlos - 51-55
   education - 52, 54-55
   family - 51-52, 54
Golden Gloves - 71
Gonzalez, Alex - 57-61
   education - 58-59, 61
   family - 57-60
   Toronto Blue Jays - 57, 59
   training - 59-60

golf - 10,
Gomez, Scott - 22
gymnastics - 8, 10
hockey - 8-9
Holyfield, Evander - 69-70
de la Hoya, Oscar - 9, 13
jockey - 18-19
   Cordero, Angel - 18
lawyers - 9, 24-25
Little League - 12, 57
Llamosa, Carlos - 63-67
   D.C. United - 64-66
   family - 63, 67
   Miami Fusion - 64
manufacturer's representative - 21
marketing director - 21, 23
Najera, Eduardo - 22
National Collegiate Athletics Association (NCAA) - 77
Nuñez, Tommy - 14
Olympics - 8-9, 12, 19
owners - 9
   baseball - 31-35
personal trainer - 23
Plunkett, Jim - 45-46, 48
public relations director - 23-24
publicist - 24, 51-55
referee - 9
Ruiz, John - 69-73
   education - 71-72
   family - 69, 72-73
   World Boxing Association (WBA) - 69
scout - 9, 23
soccer - 8-10
   Major League Soccer (MLS) - 19, 52-53, 64-66
   player - 19, 63-67
softball - 19
sportscaster - 26
sportswriter - 9, 26
swimming - 8
tennis - 8-10
track and field - 8
U.S. Olympic Committee (USOC) - 8, 77
umpire - 9
   baseball - 12
Villa, Brenda - 75-80
   education -75, 77, 80
   family - 75
   training - 76, 79-80
water polo - 75-80